We Are Our Mothers' Daughters

9 Women Who Made a Difference

Volume 1

Compiled by
Twyla Dell

Last Lap Press
2016

Dell, Twyla J. (1938-)
  We Are Our Mothers' Daughters: 9 Women Who Made a Difference
  161 p.   cm.

ISBN-13:   978-1539376552
ISBN-10:   1539376559

Volume 1: October 2016

1. Women--United States--History. 2. Mothers and daughters—
United States. 3. Women--Conduct of life. 4. Mother and child--
Anecdotes. 5. Feminism--United States. I. Dell, Twyla J. (1938-).
II. Title.

Cover photo: Twyla Dell's grandmother, Rose Platt, and mother, Alma Platt, doing her "Sweet little Alice blue gown" look—a la Teddy Roosevelt's daughter, Alice; Los Angeles, about 1920. Ninety-eight years of struggle for women's rights separate us from that moment. Onward!

Published by:
Last Lap Press
lastlappress.com
lastlappress@gmail.com
also:
weareourmothersdaughters.org
weareourmothersdaughters@gmail.com

TABLE OF CONTENTS

WE ARE OUR MOTHERS' DAUGHTERS

DEDICATION

To girls and women everywhere.
We do make the difference.

WE ARE OUR MOTHERS' DAUGHTERS

INTRODUCTION

Mothers give advice. It is the nature of the role of mother. We can't help ourselves. This collection of nine stories honors mothers whose lives have been memorable in their courage and strength, and, yes, in the advice they gave to their daughters. These mothers born in the late 19th or early to middle 20th centuries produced daughters who have taken their places at professional levels, who may have become mothers themselves, and who have lived that advice and passed their own versions on to their children.

Many of our mothers went without education because it was not available to them. Many endured the prejudice of being female. Many endured rough treatment at the hands of the men in their lives, and no laws protected them from it. Somehow they persevered and became examples of strength and endurance and even optimism. Somehow their daughters rose to fulfill their promise in more ways than their mothers could have imagined. Each daughter stood on the strong shoulders of her mother, took the advice given her for her own life and carried on her mother's spirit in fulfilling that promise.

Secretary of State Hillary Clinton closed her acceptance speech for the Democratic nomination for President, July 29, 2016, with the quote "I am my mothers' daughter and my daughter's mother!" I was touched by the triumph of that statement, how she stood on her mother's shoulders to get where she is today. I felt my own mother's story supporting my own successes. In support of Secretary Clinton's run for the White House, I have asked my friends and their friends to write their mothers' stories in support of this momentous occasion.

Please join me in rejoicing in the successes of these nine women and their mothers' stories, in their mothers' enduring strength and in the pride of fulfilling the dreams made possible by the valiant strength of the generation before them.

Pass this on to your friends, sisters, mothers, daughters— women who make a difference. The 2016 election is nothing if not about a woman being elected to the highest office in the United States. If we lose this election, it is a blow against women in this country. Another candidate may not come along for a generation and women everywhere will feel the loss.

Read this, pass it along, help get out the vote, not just for Hillary Clinton, but for women everywhere.

Twyla Dell
October 2016

1

When A Door Opens, Walk Through It

ALMA PLATT CUNNINGHAM BAIM ANDERSON

1911   —   1998

Philadelphia, Pennsylvania   Kansas City, Missouri

By Twyla J. Dell

My mother was born dead! After a long night of intense labor, she was born "black as a crow" and dead limp in a home delivery. The

doctor assessed the situation—he was almost as exhausted as my grandmother—and filled out a death certificate and left. My grandmother lay back too spent to even hold her dead child, but her aunt took the little girl by the fire and began gently rubbing and singing to her. Over time she awoke, cried, gained color and surprised everyone by living! No one was more surprised than the doctor who returned the next day, tore up the death certificate and made out a birth certificate.

WE ARE OUR MOTHERS' DAUGHTERS

At her 80th birthday Alma's children and grandchildren celebrated her "Born Dead" weekend. On her cake was written "Born Dead and Still Kickin' at 80! 1911-1991," and we sang to the tune of "Born Free:" "Born dead, dead as a door nail, dumb as a doorknob, smart as a fox!" We trailed off after that into a melee of three generations of happy hugs that she had survived! Her first walk had been through the dark birth canal from death into life. She would need that kind of grit in the years ahead.

But wait! "Dumb as a door knob! Smart as a fox!" Is that a nice thing to say about your mother? Your grandmother? She laughed when we sang it, had heard it before and relished the victory in the lyrics and the grateful hugs and kisses.

In a time when divorce was frowned on by society, my mother escaped her abusive marriage and spent years trying to shut (and lock) that door. An ongoing custody battle for my brother and me forced her to move, sometimes at a day's notice, to protect us, always wondering if we were safe. Each spot we settled in was a door we had to walk through, but Mother was there to keep us singing, dancing, laughing at her stories. Her example and encouragement was one of her enduring legacies in our lives.

Alma grew up in a home in which music flowed like a river. The whole family played an instrument or sang. We were devoted Christians and Sunday morning found every family member on stage. My grandmother Rose Platt played the piano, rolling up and down the keyboard, banging out "Onward Christian Soldiers," "Bringing in the Sheaves," and, "What a Friend We Have in Jesus." Alma sang and played a variety of instruments: a mandolin was her favorite, but also guitar, banjo, cleveite and in later years a cello.

My uncle, Ralph Platt, was a professional whistler and gave programs imitating bird calls as well as accompanying the electric organ on a hymn for the collection on Sunday morning. He once toured with Roy Rogers and Dale Evans and made an LP record with organist Loren Whitney for a company called Sacred Records in the early 1950s. Mother was proud her brother had "made it big."

My grandfather Ben Platt, born in Toledo, Ohio, in 1881, ran the collection plate. I sometimes sang with my mother. My brother

10

Bruce helped with the collection. There was never a time in my memory that my mother, my entire family was not up on stage.

The family moved from Philadelphia to Los Angeles after the flu epidemic of 1918. A neighbor of theirs had gone west and written that Los Angeles was a paradise, as indeed it must have been with orange groves marching in neat rows over the hills and dales of the valley. They settled in Eagle Rock.

When the Depression hit, Ben lost his job at the glass factory where he had worked producing Coca Cola bottles and spent the next several years digging septic tanks for families moving to the growing edges of the city. Yes, he dug holes, made the concrete lid, laid the tile to the house and field. It was a needed skill and he dug many a hole, over his head and at least a yardstick wide (I remember looking down at him standing in the hole one day using his yardstick to get the width. The hole was about 6 feet deep.) He worked by himself day after day. Mother was always embarrassed to admit what her father did, but it kept the family going.

As Alma grew, she became a natural comic. She graduated high school and got a job as a telephone operator. She told side-splitting stories of trying to connect people and being absolutely unable to do so. She wrestled with the cords and tied herself up in knots. They gave her another job of sorting cards without telling her, so she said, how to sort them. She couldn't guess what they wanted. She lost that job as well. But slowly she learned to use her left brain, learned to type and file. Always she created laughter.

As a baby, not only had she been born dead, but her brain had been hopelessly snarled by her mother's attempts to keep her from using her left hand. Grandma Rose, born in Philadelphia in 1891, tied my mother's little fist to the left side of the high chair so she was forced to use her right hand. She cried and carried on but to feed her hungry belly, to drink, to play with her food, she must do so right-handed. Alma always maintained she was addled from that experience—hence the "dumb as a door knob" description. She would say, "Turn right!" and point left. She could write upside down and backwards on the blackboard while singing a different song and tap dancing, a performance that made us all laugh. So, yes, she was addled, but only a little.

WE ARE OUR MOTHERS' DAUGHTERS

Grandma Rose regretted tying her left hand to the chair later, but at the time left-handedness was to be avoided. My own father would not allow me, also left handed, to eat at the table unless I did so with my right hand. "Dumb as a door knob, smart as a fox?" Yes, Mother was addled between left and right brains, but amazingly good at self-protection and self-promotion. She had celebrated that kind of dumb/smart attitude to the point that we all recognized and cherished both sides of her. To watch her in action, telling a story, reasoning things out was like watching a pingpong match as her brain tossed things back and forth.

In 1934, around a church potluck of tuna casserole and jello salad she met my father Jean Cunningham, a dashing and handsome milk truck driver who wore flared jodhpurs, polished knee-high leather boots and a nifty cap like a bus driver's. He looked like a young Gregory Peck. She could be forgiven for falling for him. Charming and gregarious, he had not graduated high school but had started to work for the Southern Pacific Railroad on a bridge gang at 13 to bring in family money. His father ran a cigar stand at a train station having lost his right leg in a freight elevator accident as a teenager. They had moved west from St Louis where Jean was born in 1906.

He was the second son of Andrew Jerome and Texana Cunningham. Their first, their idol, Ralph, had died of scarlet fever when he was six. Jean tried to fill that void but always felt he fell short somehow.

Jean and Alma were married February 3, 1935, in a lovely wedding at Bethel Chapel in Eagle Rock. Evangelist Essie Binkley Losie officiated. My brother Bruce was born January 7, 1936, and I was born November 8, 1938. By 1940 the couple was divorced.

The marriage had been such hell for my mother that she was willing to suffer divorce in 1940 with two babies to be a single mother when women were expected to put up and shut up. Five years of maniacal temper tantrums had driven her out. She did not mention much about it except to say that she had slept with a butcher knife under her pillow to protect herself.

We moved in with Mother's parents Ben and Rose Platt in Eagle Rock. Mother lost custody of us soon after. Jean married another woman and immediately went to court to prove that he could provide a better home and the court believed him. He came at night to pick us up, his new wife sitting in the car waiting to take care of us. He had dated her while still married. Mother and Father fought over us in the street. Mother held me. Bruce clung to her leg. Jean pulled me from her arms, Bruce from her leg. We all wailed into the night. It was my first memory. I was maybe three years old.

Jean and Alma's wedding, 1935. This is the only picture we have of the two of them together.

Jean worked for the Southern Pacific Railroad in Sacramento by then and took my brother and me with him. He had studied hard and earned his high school diploma. Took night classes in law. He rose to white-collar level quickly in the wartime atmosphere. Alma quit her job in L.A. and moved to a boarding house in Sacramento to be near us. She could see us on Sunday afternoons. Then Jean got a job in Hawthorne, Nevada, with the railroad and we left town. He did not tell Alma. For three years she did not know where we were. We simply vanished. It took her three years and a good attorney to find us.

We lived in naval barracks in Nevada—I know, it sounds like Area 51—and played with an eye to the sky for the frequent sand storms that came our way. I remember jumping from the swing a

13

running for home to slam the door before the storm hit and then watch the angry, sand-filled clouds slash and bump our house as the finest particles built up inside on the windowsill. The other storm that raged was our father's temper tantrums. He beat 8-year-old Bruce so badly he could not attend school for weeks. All those bruises had to fade away, but the outside world never knew. I learned to be invisible.

Our stepmother, fortunately, was a kindly woman, a refugee from Tennesee Dust Bowl days and willing to be married to Jean to take care of us. She was under no illusions and made no attempt to stop his temper outbursts even to protect my brother. One day she asked me if I would call her mother. I didn't know where I was or where my mother was but I knew she was out there somewhere. "I have a mother," I answered. I offered to call her Matilda—her real name was Clara--and we settled on that for years to come.

We moved back to California as the war wound down. Jean bought a house in Sacramento. Franklin Roosevelt died. All the teachers cried and school was let out. We celebrated Victory Europe Day and Victory "Jap" Day. And then, amazingly, my mother had custody of us again and we went to live with her in Monterey Park near Los Angeles.

She worked at the iconic L. A. City Hall building where people came and paid their traffic and parking tickets. She loved it because movie stars came in to pay as well. She met Clark Gable once and nearly swooned. I fell and broke my right arm and was forced to rely on my left hand! I felt so guilty using it I was almost afraid to pick up a pencil with it.

No sooner had we settled into a little house when it was broken into. Jean had hired a detective to look for proof of Alma's being an unfit mother—whatever that might look like. Liquor bottles? Cigarettes? Men's clothing? Within a day or two we were gone.

Confident that Alma was at last settled with her children, Grandpa Ben and Gandma Rose had bought 10 acres and a ramshackle cabin—horses had been the last tenants-- outside Salem, Oregon, and had just retired to have an "Egg and I" adventure, named after a book popular in the mid-1940s. By the time the 1947 movie featuring Claudette Colbert and Fred McMurray came out playing two naïve city folk who move to the country and have misadventures, we watched our own life on screen.

With the house broken into, Mother knew she had to remove us two kids from Jean's reach. Bruce and I attended the first day of school in Monterey Park. I was in the 2nd grade, he in the 4th. Fearful of losing us again, Mother plucked us from our classrooms in the middle of our first day, put us on the train and we left for Salem that evening. At no time did she let on this was anything but a gay adventure. We went with that, too, and rode the train happily into another new unknown. Another door opened; we walked through it.

Of course, Rose and Ben had not expected to double the size of their family overnight. The one-bedroom cabin they bought sat on a hill overlooking a lake. Eight miles south of Salem on gravel roads, it could be reached only by crossing two split logs over a narrow inlet of water. You had to make a run for it across the logs and up a muddy hill to swing to a stop in front of the cabin. There was a hand pump at the sink but no indoor bathroom. You reached an outhouse by balancing on a double wide of two flat boards mired in the mud! You wiped your butt on a Sears catalog page torn from a big fat dog-eared volume you could read while eliminating if you so chose. You washed your hands by priming the pump at the kitchen sink for all you were worth. My grandparents' romance with the primitive was interrupted by two scared city kids and their courageous daughter with one day's warning! Let's say our learning curve was quick and steep!

Ben immediately began to dig a septic tank and bring water into the house. My brother and I bathed in twin soapstone tubs used for laundry on the back porch. Then Ben built a bathroom indoors with a tub and a closed-in porch where Bruce slept and then built a bedroom on the back where Alma and I slept. Meanwhile, she and I hit the pull-down couch every night.

Mother enrolled Bruce and me a day or two later in a little country school about a mile down the gravel road. It was one big room divided into two by a folding plastic curtain. The "little room" contained the first four grades; the "big room" the second four grades and a stage. Two outhouses stood out back. A three sided "play barn" stood nearby so that we could play outside on the many, many rainy Oregon days.

WE ARE OUR MOTHERS' DAUGHTERS

There were four of us in the 2nd grade with a total of 64 kids in all when the school reached capacity of 8 kids X 8 grades, with one teacher per room, but most of the time the school ran at half that number. I could read and read well. Mother and Grandma Rose were both great readers, sticklers on grammar, and big on discussing what they were reading over the dinner table. It wasn't hard for me or Bruce to stand out as best scholars in our grades, though the local students did not appreciate it. The boys beat Bruce up several times and left him in a ditch. But soon after we arrived the ceiling lights began to swing and the building to sway. Bruce and I cried happily, "Oh, that's an earthquake!" Seasoned by Los Angeles tremors, we held momentary superiority.

Mother got a job with the federal government as a secretary. Post-war Salem was a busy place. Harry Truman came by in 1948 before his election against Thomas Dewey. He sat in an open car and waved. Alma said she yelled, "Hello, Harry!" And he waved at her. We listened avidly to radio news about the coming election. Grandma Rose was very political and a sincere Democrat. She thought Herbert Hoover should be hanged. We discussed the parties at length.

It was Mother's turn to take the kids and keep us away from Jean who arrived after a few months to visit. *First* he had to locate *us*! My brother and I were terrified of being taken by him again. We created a getaway in a big old stump on the property. We hid a blanket and a box of crackers and would run and hide when the occasional car bounded over the bridge and up the hill.

Ben eventually filled in the lake beneath the two shuddering logs and had a load of gravel delivered and spread on the hill so we could drive relatively sedately up to the door, but we always missed the adventure of the original ride.

Some neighbors from Tennessee moved into a little house across the road from us. They were also refugees from the Dust Bowl. Orville drove Mother to work every day. We had only one car and Ben used it to get odd jobs in town.

Orville would grind his gears at the bottom of the hill like a bull gathering for the charge, then roar into life, steering madly up the muddy, gravelly incline—he was missing a left forearm—swing to a stop, hold the steering wheel with his left stump against one of those steering knobs, fling open the door with his right hand—the door opened to the back so it always banged against the car body. He'd lean out and call, "All aboard, Buttercup!" He thought he was pretty cool!

Mother would emerge in her city clothes and daintily slip into the car. Away they would go careening down the hill, across the logs, onto the gravel road and roar into Salem a half hour away. She did that for five years.

At least twice she made the bus trip from Salem to Los Angeles to answer a court summons from Jean's attorney. It was a hard trip; she went alone and came home with adventures of sitting behind the bus driver, and having eaten a hot dog and orange juice, had thrown up down the driver's neck along the twisty curves of Grant's Pass. Now the highway is federally funded as Interstate 5, but then it was a two-lane, hair-raising strip of winding pavement. and steep grades. The driver had to pull the bus over, she said, to clean up. The bus reeked; the passengers groaned. She stood and apologized to the whole bus, and the driver reseated her farther back. We died laughing.

Somehow she staved off the law through these visits though we never received child support those five years.

When we first arrived in Oregon in September of 1945, Mother got a summons of some kind to surrender us children. She had, after all, taken us out of state without permission. We would have to run again. Rose and Ben telegraphed some friends in Little Rock, Arkansas, and asked if Alma and the kids could come and stay. We had no telephone; telegrams were a common way of communicating. We drove to Salem to send the request for help. We stood by, packed and ready, waiting for an answer. Got one back: "Yes, send them here." Then the three of us jumped on a Greyhound bus and headed east. Mother took the name Mary Cummings, Bruce became Ricky and I became Sally. We went by those names all the way across country, as we walked through another door.

We stayed about two weeks before we received another telegram that the coast was clear. We got on the bus and went back to Oregon. Occasionally, Jean would arrive unannounced to see us. Once we were driving down a street in Salem and saw him getting out of a taxi, his face red with anger as always. He had been out to the farm and we had not been home! Both Bruce and I in the back seat dropped to the floor without a word. Another time he came to the house, again taking a taxi up the long bridge, the hill, the swing around drive. Bruce and I ran to our tree stump. Dodging him became our game. We had the power now and it felt good. We didn't talk to him for five years.

Life on a small family farm kept us busy. We ate what we grew. If we had chicken on Sunday this was how we got it: Ben would go to the chicken yard and grab a hen and take it to the chopping block. With a hatchet he would do his best to get the head off with the first whack. He seldom made it in fewer than four or five. Meanwhile, Rose would go to the piano and play "Onward Christian Soldiers" as loud as she could to drown the chicken's agony. Mother would grab an instrument and play and sing along with her. The chicken head would eventually depart its body. Ben would triumphantly let the chicken go, waving his bloody hatchet. I would stand transfixed to see a chicken run around with its head cut off, which it always did.

Ben would scald the body and pluck the feathers and bring in the corpse still warm with frantic life. Rose and Alma would hold the body over an open flame. We had a huge nickel and cast-iron range we kept stoked with wood. They would lift and remove the plate and hold the hen over the open flame to burn the pin feathers. That smelled awful. Then Grandma Rose would draw the bird—open it and pull out its entrails—Mother couldn't make herself do that. Then cut off the feet, then stuff it and thrust it in the oven. From life to death to carcass to oven in a half hour or so.

We had our social times in rural Oregon. There was a farmer's grange and Rose immediately offered to play the piano on Saturday nights while the old farmers sang and danced. I made my debut singing "Some Sunday morning there's going to be . . . ." Alma played and sang. She had a fruity contralto voice and her mandolin tinkled away over songs like, "Somewhere Over the Rainbow," Red Roses for a Blue Lady," "Golden Earrings" and other songs of the day.

The school had a couple of plays per year and she starred in "The Man Who Came to Dinner," playing the part glamorous Ann Sheridan had played in the 1942 movie. The locals loved her. She was a star to the likes of rural Oregon, but she spent her 30s hiding out instead of developing her talents on larger stages, too afraid to be too obvious for fear of some form of reprisal from Jean.

**Oregon from our family hideout 1948.
Ten years later, I would be a bi-lingual college
student in Mexico City, an event no one could have
predicted. L-R: Alma, brother Ralph, Ben, Rose,
Bruce, and Twyla, 10 years old.**

By 1950, we had had the Oregon adventure. Social Security was new and paid darn little. Ben got a box of cheese every Christmas from his few years at the glass factory. His odd jobs didn't amount to much. Mother worked her secretary job. We poured everything into the common pot, but it wasn't enough. We loved Oregon. We had a huge garden in river bottom soil. Before we acquired a horse named Nellie for $25 we saved from the glue factory, Bruce and I pulled the plow ourselves up and down the rows of black earth of our immense garden.

We had milk cows named Lady and Sue, sold the milk, sold the pigs, ate the chickens, canned and ate our vegetables, picked crops for money, strawberries on our hands and knees, green beans on our haunches, picked cherries in the tree tops. Tried picking hops. They were impossible, like gathering feathers. Mother worked the crops on weekends coming home with sore fingers and knees from picking filberts, and then typed during the week. Bruce and I turned from city to country kids before we knew it. The underlying desperation we felt in this work was covered with willful good humor and hours of music. One thing Grandma Rose always had was a piano. But most of all she missed California and the sunshine. In her five-year diary she entered over and over, "Rained again today."

In June 1950, we sold the farm and bought a 24-foot Air Stream trailer and lit out for California. We had a 1938 Packard coupe—a bench seat in front with two pull-down jump seats in the back. Bruce and I sat in the back tucking our knees into the tight space.

The Packard couldn't make it up the mountainous grades of Grant's Pass with the trailer plus passengers, so four of us would get out at the bottom of a long grade and Ben would drive the straining Packard and the trailer to the top and wait for us. We would walk up, get in and ride down the hill to the next grade. We did that all the way over Grant's Pass.

In all the times, thick or thin, Mother made light of the events. She was not a complainer or a drama queen. She stepped up and did

what was necessary through every event with grace and humor! A natural raconteur, she would keep us in stitches over some misfortune of hers. I didn't realize at the time what a gift that was. Whatever depression, regret or sadness she felt she hid from us. Our conversation was upbeat, involved with whatever book she was reading—she read a lot of mysteries for a while which she would relay to us almost page for page. Always, music flowed through our lives. It was hard to be depressed when a new song, a new performance rushed toward us.

Some evenings in Oregon she would play "Encyclopedia" with Bruce and me. We could each choose a volume of the 12-book Collier's Picture Encyclopedia set of 1932 we owned—some good door-to-door salesman had convinced my grandmother she needed it, and we actually used it! We would play 20 questions, guessing what the person holding that volume might have chosen. Then we had to tell about what we had chosen. Two or three rounds of that every few weeks slowly added to our education in ways we never realized. Other times when we had a question about something, she'd say, "Look it up! Look it up!" So we learned to be independent scholars which each of us became in later years.

As I look back now, it is hard to capture what intellectual stimulation was available in the conversations between Rose, the scholar, and Alma, the delighted daughter. All manner of things were discussed. There were the great truths of the Bible that floated in and out since Grandma Rose was a great Biblical scholar and was known to correct one pastor after another as she went through life. Mother was a willing student exploring more and more New Thought realms.

There were the political truths—poor people needed help. Grandma Rose wrote many a letter to newspapers and government officials about the need for more money for retired people. Truth had a home in this house. We always spoke it with certainty. We rooted out new truths from old writings and went in quest of even deeper ones. In 1950 Immanuel Velikovsky's book, *Worlds in Collision* was

At the left: My beautiful mother, brought this low, in 1952, in the trailer on the sand dune. Outhouse out back. I don't remember how or where we bathed.

published and Grandma fell on it like a duck on a June bug. It proposed ancient catastrophies that questioned Old Testament truths! We discussed those.

We conjectured and "looked things up." Grandma Rose had a world map posted on her bedroom wall. One morning she shrieked with delight as she realized South America must surely have been part of Africa! We gathered around the map and looked it over. Who could deny such an obvious fit between the two land masses! It was not until 1968 that the scientific world accepted at last the idea of techtonic plates moving over time might have actually ripped apart these two sister continents. ((See geophysicist Jack Oliver's published article "Seismology and the New Global Tectonics," 1968, "Jack Oliver, Who Proved Continental Drift, Dies at 87". *The New York Times.* 12 January 2011. p. A16. Retrieved 6 June 2013.)) Grandma Rose knew none of the scientific literature, but she felt entitled to speculate and conjecture, to dig and analyze—basic scientific procedures open to anyone who questioned the status quo. Bruce and I learned that theories were open to anyone who wanted to know them.

Neither of these women engaged in blame, bitterness, self-pity, namecalling or other negative emotions. Unburdened by that, we were free to spend our time moving forward, learning, enjoying the give and take of discussion, humor, plays on words, vocabulary words. These two women gave us a greater gift than we could ever have imagined, and without realizing it made us ready for advanced learning.

In spite of the scramble to cover basics like food and shelter, we always knew we would some day arrive at a place of security again. We expected it sooner; it came later, but we never gave up hope. We lived and worked in expectation of better things coming.

Longing to return to sunny California, Grandma Rose had bought on time payments two 25-foot lots in Baywood Park, California, near Morro Bay and 12 miles west of San Luis Obispo. She had bought these lots "sight unseen" from a magazine ad. We left Oregon with the destination in mind to reach those lots in the summer of 1950, tried to make it to those two lots, but only got as far as Stockton where a good friend of mother's from boarding house days was a teacher there. We had run out of money completely. We parked our trailer on the back row of a trailer park on a gravel lane up against a cemetery. Mother thought that was wonderful. We spent many an hour reading gravestones and conjuring stories about the residents. She was training to be an Arthur Murray dance instructor and practiced with us on the flat stones of the departed.

Again, we were plumbing deprived and had to walk down the gravel road to use the communal toilet and showers. Mother got a job as secretary to an attorney. A couple of social security checks came in and Rose and Ben left us in the trailer for the lots in Baywood Park. That Christmas of 1950, having *no* money for gifts, the three of us wrapped up things around the house and gave them to each other. We each unwrapped an old, familiar object, made up stories about its previously unknown value, exclaimed enthusiastically about receiving it and then laughed ourselves silly.

Jean lived in Sacramento and came to visit us at the trailer park. Bruce and I stood outside the little trailer waiting for him and agreed we would only call him "Father." It was the briefest of conversations but symbolized our "profoundly superficial" relationship with him, as I came to call it. He never again raised his voice to a shrieking, spitting, red-faced outpouring of his inner demons or raised a hand to us. He didn't try to get custody again but settled for a variety of holidays and summer vacation. But he still didn't pay child support, and there seemed to be no way to make him.

Amazingly, he asked Bruce to join DeMolay and me Job's Daughters. He was now high in the Masonic Lodge in Sacramento. Without childcare expense he had money for the Masons, the Oddfellows and trips to Europe. For our fantasized debut he would buy us new clothes, a suit for Bruce and a formal for me. He wanted to show us off. We stared at him uncomprehending. We had to walk down the gravel lane to pee. We lived on another planet. Still no child support but dress up clothes to parade us around—actually how well our mother had raised us? We said no. We were not going to walk through that door so that he could show us off.

In January 1951, we made the final trek to Baywood Park. The two lots were part of a sand dune that had been bought and subdivided. Again Grandpa Ben began building a house, 24x24 feet. Four of us slept in the little trailer, Ben and Rose in the little bed behind the sliding door, Mother and I on the pull-out couch. Bruce slept on a cot in a tent nearby because there was not enough floor space for him to stretch out at night. Ben had already dug a hole and built an outhouse.

Somehow, while still in Stockton, in spite of having virtually no money, Mother had started orthodontic work on my terribly crooked teeth. I was 12. They were scandalously crooked to the point that people would squint at them when I talked. She knew I had no future like that and made it happen. Just before we left, the dentist in Stockton, oblivious of teen-age humiliation, took off the shiny metal band on one of my front teeth and said "the next dentist can fix it." So I arrived at the new school with a mouth full of braces—one of only two of us wearing them in the whole junior high--except for one naked front tooth, an "Alma-cut-it" hair cut, scuffed brown oxfords, shabby clothes. But like Mother herself, I moved on.

Mother got a job as a secretary at the California Division of Highways in San Luis Obispo. It was the best job she had had and she kept the office in stitches by painting eye balls on her eyelids with eyebrow pencil and eye shadow while she closed her eyes and typed dictation from ear phones, drew faces on her knees as the men came by to look at her shapely legs. She got a paid singing job with the Christian Science church, $6 a week. She began to come into her own. She got parts in plays being staged in the old opera house. She flourished. But a divorced woman was unwelcome in social circles, she found out. Rumor had it that she would steal your husband, too good looking for her own good. She didn't date. Our social life was church.

Ben slowly built the house—as they could afford the lumber, with one bedroom, the trailer parked out back, then eventually tacked a room on the back of the house with a Jack and Jill bathroom. Mother and I shared another bed. Finally, we had indoor plumbing, a real house. But Bruce still hung on in the tent outside. Increasingly he would stay with classmates in town and I would bring him a clean shirt each week in a paper bag and take the dirty one home.

Jean came to visit us once and looked the tent over. Laughed with Bruce over his meager digs, paid no child support. I asked him for a dollar so I could join a book club I had seen in a magazine ad. He opened his wallet choked with cash and gave me one. I looked into that wallet with no connection to that wad of cash as my birthright or privilege and neither did he. By then we had long since learned to live without him, his money, his blessing or his love.

Once I learned to type, Mother set me to work writing letters to all of the 22 Masonic lodges in Sacramento telling them that Jean Cunningham paid no child support. Eventually, Bruce's senior year, Jean sent $40 per month, one $20 bill for each of us.

The Korean War was on. Alma got her third job waitressing at night at Camp San Luis Obispo. One night she came home with all the night's proceeds in her apron pockets. She was too tired to notice. The frightened manager drove to our house to collect it. We had no phone to confirm its whereabouts. We all laughed at her as a thief!

She met and married a warrant officer, eloping to Camp Stoneman near Monterey before he was sent to Korea. He came home a year and a half later, went to L.A. to look for a job, wrote and told her he wanted a divorce—still we had no phone--and disappeared. That was the only time I heard Mother cry. She eventually got and paid for the divorce at $40 a month to some attorney in town.

Bruce graduated high school in 1954 and joined the Navy. I graduated in 1956 at 17. I expected to be a secretary like my mother, and had already done so for a couple of summers, but too young to be hired permanently I was told, I attended the local junior college for a year. While there I found a catalog to Mexico City College. It struck me like lightning that I was going to go there. Grandma Rose had always talked about the Incas, the Aztecs, the Mayas. She wanted so much to visit their sites. We had looked them up in the encyclopedias. I realized I could go for her. Borrowing a page from Mother, I opened a door and walked through it.

I left for Mexico City in September of 1958. I was 19. Mother flew down with me, saw that I had a proper place to live—in an apartment supervised by a senora overlooking the main boulevard, La Reforma. I graduated in December of 1959. I had climbed both the Aztec pyramids outside Mexico City, and had traveled by train and boat to the Mayan ruins in Yucatan. I learned Spanish, loved the country, the adventure and the challenge. Mother sent me $50 a month. She bought me a green Underwood portable typewriter so I could type my papers. Father also sent $50 for room and board. He bought me a 35mm camera from which I have pictures of me on top of the ruins at Chichen Itza. I earned the tuition money myself my freshman and sophomore year.

For the first time I had a bed to myself as a junior in college. Mother and I had huddled together all those years and in doing so had protected each other's chastity, and shielded each other from the wider world. I don't know if it ever occurred to her to bring home a man and send me to the living room to sleep, but she never did.

That neighbor from Philadelphia who had urged the family to move to Los Angeles had always been in contact. Fred Anderson asked my recently widowed grandmother to wed. She accepted, sold the little beach bungalow Ben had built and moved back to her beloved Los Angeles.

Mother got reacquainted with her childhood playmate, Al Anderson, Fred's son, and soon they were married—mother and daughter marrying father and son!

Now the fun began. All the years of privation were over. Mother worked as a secretary for the state of California in Los Angeles. Al worked in Long Beach in harbor repair—he was a carpenter—a 'wood butcher' as he called it. They moved into a nice mobile home park—they were no

Alma and husband, Al Anderson, at their best in the 1970s with their musical career in full swing.

longer called trailer parks. Holidays were gala affairs with more rollicking music than you could keep in one house!

Al and Alma served as social directors of the park and were on stage at least once a week. Al played the banjo. They both sang. They were a hit.

They had a five-piece band with band stands and were invited to play on the Queen Mary in the port at Long Beach for New Year's Eve for 10 years in a row. And of course there was always Sunday morning.

Mother died of dementia in 1998. Al had died of a heart attack in 1987. Jean died in 1989 of prostate cancer. Neither Bruce nor I could shed tears for a man who never apologized for his heartlessness.

Mother's greatest gift was her unassuming courage. She didn't seem to be afraid of much of anything, and every obstacle was a new adventure. Although the phrase "going to college" never passed anyone's lips—that's what people with money did--against all odds Bruce and I both graduated college, each working our way through, and have lived successful lives—I as a high school teacher, seminar leader and author, and Bruce as business owner and student of physics--due to our mother's consistent interest in our intellectual side—grammar, vocabulary—she was the queen of exotic words—"Callipygian" comes to mind (As Alma would say, "Look it up!")—reading, story telling, discussion and general brave inquisitiveness.

Some might have said we could not go to college. The high school counselors certainly didn't expect two children from a divorced, single mother who lived in a trailer on a sand dune to do so. I am one of two Ph.D.s from a high school class of over 200. But, we didn't know we couldn't! Hadn't we already proved we could handle whatever life threw at us? Our mother certainly had. We followed her example. She looked a cruel life in the eye and laughed, danced and sang her way through it. She bravely opened and walked through every door.

WE ARE OUR MOTHERS' DAUGHTERS

  Twyla Dell was born in Los Angeles in 1938, graduated from San Luis Obispo High School in California in 1956, thought she should be able to go to college in spite of no money and made it happen. She received her B.A. from Mexico City College, now the University of Americas in Puebla, Mexico, in 1959. Returning to one of her earlier stops toward adulthood, she spent a graduate year earning a general secondary teaching credential in 1961 at University of Pacific in Stockton, CA. In Virginia in 1978 (taken by first husband's cross-country transfer) she received her master's degree in English from George Mason University, Fairfax, VA, and left teaching for writing and editing in Kansas City (another transfer). She was fortunate enough to spend two short years in public affairs at the U.S. Environmental Protection Agency in Kansas City before Ronald Reagan came in and declared trees caused air pollution. Before she was RIFFED (*reduction in force* to weaken environmental regulations and staff power.), the new divorcee met her second husband-to-be at EPA the first week on the job.

  In 1990, moved by the growing environmental calamity of burning rainforests--this issue was the global climate change of the 1990s--she designed a weekend experiential environmental leadership program (ELP) for Kansas City business and community leaders, teachers and students, educating them to look at a larger picture than EPA regulations on water and air quality.

Her company, The Foresight Institute, offered that retreat-style learning experience for 5 years. She and colleague Kelly Ellison also founded 45 high school chapters of Rainbow Generation, an after-school environmental program around Kansas City used by high school science teachers.

Looking for new ways to continue her environmental work, she enrolled in the graduate school at Antioch University New England in Keene, New Hampshire, to look at fuel and energy patterns from wood age, to coal age to oil age to solar age in particular in and around Kansas City from 1820 to 1920. She is now adding the 20th and 21st centuries to that narrative with fresh research and will soon publish an updated volume: "Wood Piles to Wind Turbines: 200 Years of Kansas City's Fuel and Energy Story." (Honestly, it's more interesting than it sounds!) She graduated with a Ph.D. in environmental studies in 2009 at the age of 70, fifty years after her 1959 B.A. from Mexico City. (How far from that trailer on the sand dune).

She lives with her 92-year-old husband, Carl Blomgren, who retired from EPA Region VII as water division director. Two sons work professionally in Texas and California and together have four grandchildren. Colleague Kelly Ellison counts as their daughter and also has a child who calls them Papa and Nana.

WE ARE OUR MOTHERS' DAUGHTERS

2

To Really Know Yourself, You Must Know Where You Came From and Who Your Forefathers and Mothers Were

CHARLOTTE LEWIS PATTEN

October 16, 1921 — April 22, 1997

by Cherie Patten Post Dargan

My mother, Charlotte Lewis Patten, was born on a farm in the rolling hills of central Iowa that her great-great grand- father had settled on in 1855. Her parents were Lee Ward and Nellie Lorena Lewis. My mother was one of three daughters--the middle child--and her two sisters, Reva and Jeanne, were her life-long friends. She came from a family of pioneers, storytellers and hard workers, and taught us to value our family history, our faith, and each other.

Charlotte in the 1970s in a publicity photo for her devotional writing.

31

WE ARE OUR MOTHERS' DAUGHTERS

Charlotte's great grandparents on both sides were early settlers in Tama County. One grandfather—Dr. Hiram Welton—was an herb doctor and author, while another was a blacksmith. Nellie's father, Robert Filloon, fought in the Civil War with a regiment out of Tama County. Lee's grandparents, Frank and Diana, lost their first child at the age of two, and then adopted a little French immigrant's son and later his sister. That little boy, Frank Lewis, grew up to marry Eva Dutton, and their son Lee became Charlotte's father.

Nellie's parents (Ransom and Ethel) were born in Iowa but moved out west to homestead in Missouri and Colorado as well as Washington. The marriage ended and Ethel and her three girls took the train back to Iowa to live with her mother's family. Nellie missed her father and her brother Charley, who was forced to stay with his father. She was sent from relative-to-relative to work and earn her keep once she turned 12. She met Lee at the country school where he left love notes in her desk. They married in 1913; she was 16…he was 17.

Lee worked as a farmhand when he married Nellie: they rented a little house and he bought a worn out race horse, named him Charlie, and rode him to his jobs. The following year, Lee bought more farmland from his brother, for a total of 160 acres. Lee cut down many loads of wood from the timber to buy his bride a wedding ring, silverware and a big table to furnish their house, which his mother had built ten years earlier. He farmed and bought two trucks to haul livestock.

Nellie gave birth to Reva, the oldest daughter, and two years later, my mother was born. Almost four years passed, and the two little girls were playing in the yard one sunny July day when their Papa came out and said, "Girls, you have a brand new baby sister!" Five-and-a-half-year old Reva was amazed: "Does Mama know?" she asked, which amused Lee and Dr. Launders, who arrived to deliver the baby in the early morning hours.

Nellie had a large vegetable garden, chickens, a farm house and three children to look after, but she loved to walk in the nearby timber and gather flowers, and listen to the birds singing. She loved to read the Bible and poetry, in spite of a limited education. When I went off to college, Grandma Nellie would use a small cassette player to record a message to me: it was easier than writing letters, but it was funny to play her tapes and have people peek in my dorm room to see where I was hiding the chickens, pigs, or birds they were hearing.

Lee took the family out west in 1927: a friend built a truck house on one of his large farm trucks. They placed several mattresses and a big cedar chest inside, loading the big chest with their goods, put their furniture into storage and sold some equipment. His mother, Eva, went along and the family enjoyed the adventure, first going to Kansas to visit relatives and then to Colorado, where my mother remembered visiting people in adobe houses. They continued on to California, where they visited Aimee Semple McPherson's temple, named after the renowned woman evangelist, went to the San Diego zoo, and admired the ocean.

They started the journey home heading first to Arizona: fortunately, they met someone else traveling in a truck house because when the big trucks got stuck in the sandy desert, the men took turns digging each other out. My mom remembered taking pictures by prickly cactus barrels, under Joshua trees, and beside rocky mountain peaks. They reached Phoenix and stayed there for a few weeks in a little campground before finding a small bungalow to rent for a few months. Her father found work digging ditches and laying pipe while her grandmother worked as a housekeeper for someone near Camelback Mountain.

Her father made friends with a Mr. Wheeler who took pictures for the *National Geographic* and was a stunt man on airplanes, so on Sundays they went to the airport to watch small planes do "loop the loop" and other tricks. Once she and Reva got to take a ride with their father and Mr. Wheeler in a small plane that had open windows: her sister said, "Please don't do any loop the loops!"

Reva and Charlotte went to the little Phoenix school near their house for three months in the winter/spring of 1927/1928. In April they started for home, stopping at the Grand Canyon, the Petrified Forest, Painted Desert, and the great meteor crater. My mother remembered Grandma Eva taking her hand and walking up close to the edge of the Grand Canyon, while her mother protested in the background. Charlotte was never afraid of heights after that!

They got back to Iowa, rented a house in Garwin, and enrolled the two older girls in school, with Charlotte in first grade, and life returned to normal. In 1933 they visited the World's Fair in Chicago where Grandma Eva had moved. She was doing practical nursing, taking care of young mothers and their babies. Then a few months later in 1933 Lee died of tetanus, commonly known as "lock jaw" because of the tightening of the muscles around the face and neck, after cutting his finger on a rusty can.

This left his young family in desperate condition when the company holding his insurance policy wouldn't pay. They moved into Garwin and rented out the farm; however, the renter did not pay the rent on a regular basis. Nellie asked her brother to help with the trucking business but it failed after she could not keep up with the payments on one of the trucks.

Several years later Nellie married a family friend, Arthur Egger, who had also driven one of the trucks for Lee. Grandma Eva moved back from Chicago to help the family.

Charlotte was just 12 when her father Lee died and she grieved terribly. However, everyone had to work to survive so they grew and tended a big garden, and the older girls found part time jobs. Charlotte spent a couple of hours a day looking after an older man in town. She graded papers and did office work for the superintendent. She graduated from Garwin High School with honors and then went up to Cedar Falls to study at the Teachers College, where they had an

Miss Lewis with children at the Rock Valley Country School, Carleton Township, Tama County, Iowa, 1941/2.

abbreviated program. She took her tests and got her teaching credentials for Normal School.

Charlotte taught at the Rock Valley country school, located adjacent to the family farm, from 1941-1944. She kept a journal, recording the nervousness she felt in the early weeks of teaching, calling herself Miss Lewis, School Marm. She wrote about the growing war in Europe and the shock and anger felt by Americans after the Japanese attack on Pearl Harbor, recognizing that many of he r friends and former classmates would be going to war.

Both of her sisters were married by now: her younger sister Jeanne and husband Wendell went to California to work in an air craft factory, while big sister Reva was living near a military base in Red Bank, New Jersey where Lester was stationed. Charlotte got letters from Wendell and Lester in the spring of 1944, telling her she was going to be an aunt and asking her to visit. Lester was about to be deployed overseas; Wendell was concerned that Jeanne had been sick with her pregnancy. So, Charlotte did not renew her teaching contract for the fall of 1944; instead, she organized her travel plans, first taking the train to New Jersey in the early weeks of summer. There she settled in at a boarding house where her sister lived, got work at a bakery for a few months to pay her way, and helped her sister prepare for the new baby. She made friends at the bakery, where her boss nicknamed her "Teacher," telling the others to watch while Charlotte carefully filled donuts with jelly! She enjoyed living out east, and took several trips to New York City and Washington, D. C.

Summer turned to fall, and her mother wrote and said she was worried about Jeanne out in California, who was due in November, so Charlotte packed her bags and took the train back to the Iowa farm for a short visit before going out to California in October. Her journal is filled with stories about her adventures on those train trips—meeting young couples who had just married before the husband was deploying for war, talking to soldiers on the train, and watching the scenery pass by. She fell asleep one night and woke to discover a thoughtful soldier had draped his coat over her; at the end of the trip, he helped her get her suitcase off the train and made sure she met her friend before leaving.

WE ARE OUR MOTHERS' DAUGHTERS

Charlotte spent the first four days in North Hollywood with Pauline, an old friend from Iowa. Pauline's husband sang in a gospel quartet, and had practice that night, but his car was being repaired, so they were getting a ride with another quartet member named Harry, a young carpenter who had also worked in an aircraft factory. Pauline so Charlotte went along. Charlotte was very impressed with Harry, who was tall, handsome and very courteous. The quartet called themselves *The Gospel Light* quartet and they sang on the radio in Hollywood, California. Harry found a reason to visit every day during Charlotte's visit and told her that he wanted to marry her on their last day together.

However, now it was time to go help her younger sister in San Diego, about 130 miles away. Jeanne and Wendell were happy to see her, and she settled into their little house in National City. Charlotte got a job at Rohr aircraft where she enjoyed working: she wrote about her job assembling cowl rings in her journal. When her nephew, Jimmy, arrived earlier than planned, she took time off work to help with the baby. In the meantime, Harry wrote her letters, sent her a lovely locket and came to visit. As the war came to an end, the air-craft factory work slowed down significantly because of a shortage of parts.

She moved to North Hollywood in 1945 and worked at J. C. Penney's until she and Harry married in February of 1946. Almost a year later, my big sister Cathi was born in 1947, with a congenital hip deformity that meant she had to be in a full body cast and then wear braces. My mother's deeply intuitive, spiritual side prompted her to go check on baby Cathi one day: the toddler had somehow gotten a screw loose from her crib and was choking on it! She picked up Cathi, turned her over, slapped Cathi on her back and the screw popped out of her mouth. She always told us girls she thought an angel had put the thought into her mind to check on the baby and to listen to that little voice.

Charlotte and Harry returned to Iowa in 1950, where he found work as a carpenter. They spent the first six months living in the schoolhouse. They moved into town and became involved with the local church she attended as a teenager. My father became a deacon and taught the adult Bible study class while my mother became the superintendent of the Sunday school program. He also organized a

Bible quiz program for the teens, and wrote and directed the annual Christmas program.

She was also busy taking care of little Cathi and wanted to add to their family. Unfortunately, she had several miscarriages. One night she was reading the Bible and praying when she sensed an inner voice asking what she wanted: she said, "Oh, Lord, I want a baby!" My parents had already completed an application to adopt a child when she discovered she was pregnant. Her doctor put her on bed rest and she carried me almost full term: I was born a month early. My sister, almost 7 years older, loved to say that she had to scrub floors when mother was on bed rest; however, women from the church helped with the housework and brought in meals. From all of the pictures, it is clear that I was a very spoiled baby who adored her parents and big sister.

As I grew up, we spent time at my grandparents' farm almost every Sunday afternoon. We walked out to the farmyard to see the horse, cows, and pigs. I picked flowers and loved swinging in the swing in the willow tree in the yard by the house. We went down into the cool storm cave. My sister and I didn't like the old fashioned outhouse, however, and were happy when grandma got her indoor bathroom.

Harry and Charlotte on their Honeymoon at Laguna Beach, California, in 1946.

My mother got a full time job at Kiowa, a factory, in 1964. She worked in the tool crib, organizing and maintain-ing tools that people checked in and out. She saw firsthand how poorly women were treated at the factory, and got involved with the UAW.

Soon she was the secretary and helped with their newsletter. Later, Charlotte became the 2nd vice president and served as interim president for two months due to the promotion and illness of the two higher officers. She wrote, "It was a most interesting experience and I learned even more good things about my union. It is the most active and effective protector of the rights of the elderly and common citizens." She traveled to Washington D.C. with a group of UAW officers and met Jimmy Carter when he was running for president in 1976. They were at a big UAW meeting, where she also met Ted Kennedy. I have pictures of her with both men: they all look so young.

Charlotte joined the board of the local Visiting Nurses association. She became an advocate for children, women and senior citizens. She also gave blood whenever asked; she had an unusual blood type and would get phone calls from the hospital when someone came in needing that kind of blood.

My Mother at Kiowa, in her tool crib.

While a conservative Christian in some ways, she was also a feminist and strong Democrat. She wrote a lot of letters to the editor to express her opinion on a variety of issues. She worked with her Union for various political campaigns. She was in favor of abortion rights and once in the middle of a family meal said that if her daughter got raped, she would want her to have the choice of having an abortion. The whole table got quiet and someone said quietly, "go grandma!"

Charlotte didn't get a college degree when she got her teaching credentials in 1940, which she regretted. She took several courses through Drake University and exceled. However, due to their cost, she stopped taking college courses. She was a natural teacher and taught me to read before I went to school; she typed up stories on her old Smith Corona typewriter and then used her sewing machine to put the pages together and create little readers for me.

My father dropped out of high school to help his father's construction company, and finished his degree in night school. He had nott been able to go to college either; however, they were voracious readers and had excellent vocabularies. They also did public speaking at church, and my mother went out in the community to do talks about her travels.

My parents instilled a love of reading in us: Christmas and birthday presents almost always included books and we read aloud as a family. My mother told me that she once got so engrossed in a story that she let the peas burn on the stove, and got a good scolding. My parents were always reading a book: we got the daily paper and several magazines.

Charlotte always loved to write and started to do research on our family; she and my father drove all over Iowa to courthouses and cemeteries to gather information. She talked to her aunts, cousins, her mother and grandma Eva and recorded their family stories. She put together a family tree, decades before ancestry.com existed. Charlotte had been given old scrapbooks, photos, legal documents, and other keepsakes from several generations, as well as old aprons and linens and quilts.

When I was a senior in high school in 1972, my parents took a trip that changed their lives: they went on a 17-day trip that included stops in London, Rome, Athens, Lebanon, Egypt and Israel. They saw King Tut's tomb and toured ancient temple ruins with giant columns. They sampled a lot of exotic foods and made friends. They especially enjoyed the tour in Israel: my mother took a lot of pictures and my father admitted to capturing a little of the Red Sea in an empty pill bottle.

I have a wonderful picture of Charlotte and Harry posing with some Egyptian porters, and they're all smiling. One of the other pictures of that trip shows Charlotte up on a camel's back. Apparently the camel driver hadn't made enough money that day because my father had already paid for mom's camel ride, but had to borrow money from our pastor to pay for getting her down afterward! She wrote a paper after the trip to get college credit, and was asked to write devotionals for *God's Word for Today*, a national publication by Gospel Publishing House.

After High School graduation in 1972, I went to Central Bible College in Springfield, Missouri. That move was a difficult adjustment for my parents. My sister and brother-in-law lived across the street from them. Their son, my nephew David, was growing up fast. My grandma Nellie started to have health problems; they had moved her into town after Grandpa Art died, She lived in a little house next door to them. My grandma loved her little house filled with her antique furniture, pictures, and treasures. When she needed more help, they moved her into my parents' house.

After two years of college, I dropped out to marry C. A., a young man going into the ministry. My mother was very supportive, but now that I am older, I look back and think that I must have broken their hearts. Both of my parents wanted to go to college, but family problems and World War II prevented them from following their dreams. I loved college, got almost straight A's, and naively believed that I would be able to continue my education once married and moved. (Instead, it would take a decade).

My husband and I moved to Newport, Rhode Island, to take over a tiny Home Missions church: Newport was a Navy town and once the naval fleet moved, most of the church members moved as well. My parents came to visit us frequently in Newport, and my father started to bring his carpentry tools to help us. Grandma Nellie came several times as well. My father spent one summer with us, turning our parsonage back into one home: it had been two apartments when we moved in, and we lived on the second floor. Then my mother came and helped me put up sheer curtains in my lovely new dining room.

She was also a wonderful grandmother, flying out to help me with both of my babies. My first baby, Michelle, was actually ten days late: my parents held off flying out but finally decided to come for Easter weekend. I went into labor during Sunday morning service and left the house in tears because I had smelled my mother's wonderful pot roast dinner and realized that I would not get to eat any! She stayed with us for several weeks to help.

Four generations: Baby Michelle, author Cherie, mother Charlotte and grandmother Nellie, 1980, in Newport, R.I., parsonage dining room.

My second child, Daniel was born 2 ½ months early: I had problems with my pregnancy and was diagnosed with placenta previa. I was admitted to the high-risk maternity unit at Women's and Infants Hospital in Providence, R. I. at 6 ½ months after losing the mucous plug and leaking amniotic fluid. My mother called: she dreamed I was calling for her. Mom had tickets to fly from Iowa to help with Mikki (Michelle) and the new baby.

Before saying goodbye, she asked, "You aren't bleeding, are you?" I said "No," and hung up the phone; however, my nurse came in to check me and found that I was bleeding. My mom's dream prepared her to come out to help us much sooner than planned. I was my mother's daughter and had been having a strange dream all fall—that I would have the baby too soon, in a strange hospital, with new doctors and nurses that I did not know. My dream prompted me to review my Lamaze notes and make a list of what to pack for the hospital after I started having problems at 6 ½ months: my husband used the list the next day.

My mother was there within a couple of days of Daniel's birth. Even though she had a heart condition and arthritis, Charlotte moved in to the guest room and took over, helping my minister husband with the house and caring for three-year-old Michelle. For three months she became a surrogate mother to my daughter so that I could stay with friends near the hospital. She gave stability to my little girl when she needed it so badly, and she gave me the ability to focus on my son fighting for his life. She was there with us in the Neonatal Intensive Care Unit on Christmas day when he was not quite two weeks old. She got to hold him and marveled at his tiny body. After 2 ½ months, he was transferred down to our local hospital: I was able to go in and breastfeed him and finally he came home. She stayed a little longer, until I was able to handle things. I missed her so much when she left.

When I think about my mother, I realize that she taught by example: I grew up in the early days of black and white TV and can remember her watching Jack La Lane and getting down on the floor to exercise with him. She taught me to cook and clean. Mom used to say the quickest way to get a clean house was to have company coming over!

She loved to cook and feed people: after she started working at Kiowa, she relied on a few things like TV dinners and Kentucky Fried Chicken, but still made her wonderful pot roasts and other meals on the weekend. She enjoyed stocking the freezer and making my father's sandwiches up for the week. She was very fond of purple grape juice, chocolate, especially Hershey bars, and marshmallow chocolate cookies. She made wonderful soups, cookies, pies, and all kinds of jello salads.

I watched her care for her aging mother and grandmother: taking them food, taking them to doctors' appointments, and checking on the nursing home where my great-grandma finally died. I went with her and my grandmas to the two family cemeteries several times a year to care for the family graves; we walked around and talked about the people buried there. ("That's your great-great-grandfather, who fought in the Civil War.")

I watched her be the best grandmother to my children and to David, my nephew. She read stories, she bought a little phonograph and records, she praised and showed affection and helped support my efforts, whether it was "potty" training or learning to read or do math.

I watched my mother work at the dining room table, as she put together her Christmas programs and articles. I think she invented copy and paste—she would type things up and cut them into strips (each strip with one piece to recite for the Christmas program, or a paragraph of an article or devotion) and then rearrange them until she liked the order, and use rubber cement to place them on a new sheet of paper.

Charlotte loved the technology of her day, and while we were not wealthy, she owned a camera, movie camera, slide projector, movie projector, and large reel-to-reel tape recorder and had one of the first word processors. She took movies and pictures of special occasions, and recorded us on her tape recorder. She created slideshows of her travel adventures and gave presentations. If she were alive today, she would want an iPad, laptop, iPhone, and WiFi.

Her mother and stepfather Art deeded the little schoolhouse to Charlotte. After Art's death, my parents worked on the school house for almost a decade, creating four nice bedrooms and a bathroom upstairs. The building she had taught in had burned down and been rebuilt, but the school house became a lovely rural home, with lots of dad's signature built-ins, a big garage with a workbench, a second floor deck over the garage, and a big garden that looked down on the old family farm. They finally moved out to the schoolhouse in 1984.

Growing up, my parents had a dog that died, but after moving to the country, my mother took in several little stray cats. Soon, she had several adult cats and several litters of kittens; we have a picture of my father Harry holding a big cardboard box on his lap full of kittens! My father built her a little cat-house room, divided into several smaller rooms, including a small screened-in porch where Charlotte sat on a lawn chair and held her kitties. They had a big garden, enjoyed the view of the old farm and rolling hills, and lived there for almost 15 years.

Charlotte in her late 60's, with a favorite calico, sitting at her schoolhouse in rural Garwin, Tama County, Iowa.

Both of my parents took early retirement/ disability after serious injuries. In 1974 my father was in a construction accident, when a large trussed roof collapsed on him; he said later that he heard a voice say "Harry, put on your hard hat and get on your knees." That saved his life, even though he had some crushed vertebrae. My parents' strong faith in God helped them through his difficult recovery. My mother was in a serious car accident that injured her neck and back and developed diabetes and arthritis. She took disability in 1981 after almost 18 years at the factory.

After my Aunt Jeanne and Uncle Wendell began to go out to Arizona for the winter, my parents followed. They bought a little trailer out there in a court filled with Iowans that included some of her cousins. Charlotte ended up having hip replacement surgery there and loved the University hospital staff. Her sister and brother in law took good care of her. My parents also got involved with a local church that had a prison ministry, going into a large prison on a regular basis.

Charlotte loved it in Tucson: she decorated their trailer, planted a few plants, did lots of socializing, and focused on her writing. She acquired her first word processor after using her trusty old manual typewriter for years. She began to correspond with an old childhood friend, Bruce, and they exchanged chapters detailing their lives. She made photocopies of her letters to him, so we still have those, as well as his replies. She also busied herself getting all of her family stories written up and placed into big notebooks, along with photos and obituaries, telegrams, legal papers, and other materials. My father always took his tool box along, to help the "older people" with a few repairs. They found a great deal of happiness there.

In 1982, shortly after the birth of our second child, we accepted an invitation to become the assistant pastor at my home church just a few months later, and we moved back to Marshalltown, Iowa, and ended up living in the little house where grandma Nellie had once lived next door to my parents. Michelle, 3, would go next door for breakfast: there was a little gate in the fence between us, and she would ring the doorbell to the delight of "Grandma Char." My sister lived across the street, so our three families were on one short block.

When we moved to Iowa, Danny was just six months old but the size of a newborn, and had some respiratory issues that first winter, so my mother and Cathi and I would take turns sitting up with him in the rocker. We felt so close. We would load up the car and go to the grocery store and end up with 17 bags of groceries between us; fortunately, mom had a giant Ford Galaxy with a big trunk and we would laugh as the young man from the store got our bags stowed away.

Unfortunately, those happy days did not last: my husband left the ministry and then us. When my marriage ended, my mother was my biggest supporter. We had gone to marriage counseling and our counselors had encouraged me to go back to college; I was now a junior at Buena Vista College in Marshalltown. My mother grieved with me over the divorce, gave me her car to go to college and watched my children. Many weekends my parents came to town, loaded up the children for an overnight visit, and gave me time to study, clean, and go out on a few dates.

My mother was rewarded when she attended my graduation ceremony in Storm Lake for Buena Vista; I graduated Cum Laude with a double Bachelor of Arts in English and Psychology, a minor in education, and my teaching credentials in 1987. Two years later, she and my father saw me graduate from Iowa State University with my master's degree in English composition and rhetoric. I got a full-time job at a community college in Sioux City, developing curriculum a few months later, then the governor cut the budget and my full-time job became a part-time job. My children came back to the schoolhouse for the summer and started school in Garwin and Green Mountain while I finished up my job and moved our household possessions back.

My mother took my daughter—now in middle school—to cheerleading practice and my father took my third-grade son to boy scouts. The children played with the cats, helped in the garden, rode the school bus, and kept up with their church friends on Sunday. They adjusted better than I did! When I finally moved back, it was to my parent's schoolhouse while we waited for an apartment to open up. However, now that I am a grandmother myself, I understand how remarkable it was for my parents to become surrogate parents for almost six months in their late 60's. They never complained, and then joked that it made them feel young.

We moved into our apartment and my parents went to Arizona for some badly needed rest that winter. I juggled several part time adjunct jobs with subbing; finally, I got a job as a full time technical writer for a major insurance company in Des Moines. I missed the classroom and finally got a full time teaching job at Hawkeye Community College in Waterloo in 1996.

My mother struggled against great odds with her health. She developed heart problems, diabetes, and was in pain from her neck and back injuries. She had a stroke and recovered with therapy. She seemed indestructible and had so much to live for. She wrote once that she had a lot of stories that were crying out to be written.

Above all, my mother loved her family, children and grandchildren. She took great pride in her grandson David becoming a minister and attending his wedding; she loved his wife, also named Charlotte, and their three children. She grieved when her older sister died and became even closer to Jeanne, who is now 93.

Unfortunately, my mother died all too soon, in April of 1997, after a car accident returning from wintering in Arizona. My father fell asleep at the wheel and the car went into a ditch: it is a miracle they both survived. Several weeks later a blood clot exploded in her bowel: they did surgery but she slipped into a coma during recovery, and died a few days later. She was only 75 so it was shocking.

Several retired farmers came to her funeral and introduced themselves as her former students at that little country school house. Men and women from the factory and her old Union friends were there as well as several women from the Visiting Nurses. I heard some wonderful stories about her.

Charlotte was buried in Turner cemetery not far from the family farm and schoolhouse, and near the graves of her parents, sister, and grandmother as well as many other family members. My father died in 2013, at 95, and they are buried side by side in this peaceful little country cemetery.

I learned so much from this amazing woman, with her strong opinions about politics, her passion for family history, and love of family. Charlotte left behind many albums of family history, with photos and detailed stories on each relative, a number of notebooks with her correspondence, and numerous photo albums. I listened to her stories, as well as those of my grandma Nellie and Aunt Jeanne while growing up, but I am so thankful that my mother took the time to write them down for my children and grandchildren.

Reading through her journals and letters I discovered each generation has had its own challenges, from homesteading to war, the Depression, loss of a child or spouse, divorce, death, and poverty. However, we come from stubborn, hardworking people who do not give up. My mother was a brilliant woman without a college degree working in a factory who wanted to be a writer, and she saw half a dozen sets of her devotionals published in *God's Word for Today*, as well as leaving behind numerous journals, letters and family history.

I struggled to get my education and raise my children as a single parent, and it was my mother and sister who helped me reach my goals. Each generation of pioneers, storytellers and hard workers has encouraged the next one to appreciate our family history, renew our faith, and help each other.

Cherie Dargan is her mother's daughter: a teacher, a writer, a family historian, and now a grandmother.

"My two grandsons, Corbin and Mason, are the eighth generation of our family born in Iowa. Having taken early retirement this fall, I'm babysitting my three-year-old grandson, Mason, one day a week, and each time I do, I think of my mother, her help when my children were younger, and what a wonderful grandmother she was to my children. In addition, I am working on plans for a series of books that incorporates some of my mother's stories.

"I know who I am from hearing and reading my mother's stories, and I am now the storyteller. I am a person of faith, an advocate for education, and fascinated by how social media, mobile technology, and the internet have changed our world. I am also a strong democrat and thrilled to be voting for our first female Presidential candidate. I wish my mother were alive and could see Hillary's campaign speeches and commercials; she would be enthusiastic, too, and she would be down at the UAW Hall making phone calls for the election and updating her Facebook page on her iPad."

WE ARE OUR MOTHERS' DAUGHTERS

3

If You're Gonna Make a Mistake, Make It LOUD!

PATRICIA JANE PUNNELL DURIE

August 8, 1926 — July 12, 2002
Marshall, Minnesota   Boise, Idaho

By Jane E. Frederick

My mother always said, "If you're gonna make a mistake, make it loud!" The first time I heard her say this to me, she was referring in general to the practice of theater, music and art. I was probably auditioning for a play or singing in a solo competition and she wanted to encourage me. However, this is truly how Patricia Durie, the woman who was my mother, lived her life. She was loud, colorful, silly and fun. She had learned young how to make a splash in the world and make what could have looked like a mistake into a magnificent interlude. She was an awesome soul. Every event, large or

small, was a scene leading up to something, telling a part of the story, revealing the character and the light and love of the character she was playing in the grand show called her life.

Patricia was raised in a small town in South Dakota established in the late 1800's. My grandparents, William and Dottie Punnell, were merchants selling socks, and hats and coats and fulfilling the everyday needs of the people of this small town after the stock market crashed in the early 20th century. The business was prosperous in spite of the economic downturn in the country. Patricia was the youngest of four children. My grandparent's first child Esther, died very young. Her brother Bill was born in 1917 and was a fighter pilot in World War II and would be shot down and killed in the air battle for Midway Island. Her sister Katherine was born in 1919 and then Patricia was born in 1926.

I know my mother's family had money probably because the need for hats and coats and other such things remained constant in spite of the country's serious economic struggles. Patricia was able to attended college in Minneapolis after high school and intended to become a nurse. But she could not stand the needles, or the blood. What Patricia really wanted to do was play music professionally. She loved music and theater and was a prolific writer. She wrote poems, short stories, and musical pieces for the piano. Life took a slightly different turn for her however. She quit college and married Chuck Stauffer, and then became pregnant soon after.

I do not know what her parents thought of him and I have little to tell about how they met. It is not a story I ever heard. However, I do know that Chuck Stauffer was a mistake. But like Patricia always said, "Make it Loud!" So loud it was. This mistake was part of the development of the character (the main character in her story) and represented a crucial turning point in her life. Without that mistake, Patricia would never have had Susan (my sister Susie), and she never would have embarked on the adventure that led her to Boise, Idaho, the town which would become the setting for the rest of her story and become her home for the rest of her life.

The story goes that Chuck Stauffer ran off and left Patricia with a baby. What made her chase that man down to Las Vegas with baby in tow, we will never know. The fact that my mother was very persistent and determined in everything she started hints at the motivation behind her decision. She did not like to leave things undone! Once in Las Vegas, she found an unseemly and unwelcoming environment and hopped back on the train to go home to South Dakota. Perhaps it was pride, perhaps it was the pretty trees, but she decided not to ride all the way back, but instead got off the train in Boise, Idaho.

I can't imagine a woman in the late 1940's making a decision to be alone in an unknown town and caring for a baby. Abandoned by her husband and left to fend for herself – but I imagine Patricia made a show of it. For her, everything was part of the show. It was all a great drama and somewhere there was triumph to be found. Patricia got a job and found a home with a local family in an upstairs apartment and proceeded to raise her daughter as a single mom.

Patricia made it on her own for many years and from everything I've heard, Patricia's fierce independence kept her and Susie fed and clothed and provided a home. When my grandparents retired in the 1950's, they bought a house in Boise and joined my mother and Susie as residents of Boise. My aunt followed as well. As far as I know, Patricia always maintained her own home and did not live with her parents. She also found time to write and play music and participate in church activities.

When Patricia joined the little theater and became part of a company called the Eichman Corale in the mid-50's she met my father, Andrew Durie. Susie was 11 years old when they married.

I do know that after my mother and father were married, the world changed dramatically for my mother and sister. He became comfortable and out came the booming, yelling voice. He was very obsessive compulsive and once they were married, that beast came out regularly. I think there are things you think of as normal when you are exposed to them all your life. This behavior was normal for my brother and me, but this was not true for my mother and Susie. While their life together before my father may have had its unstable elements, I imagine it was pretty quiet as Mother was not a yeller. I know my sister loved my dad. When the obsessions and bosiness came about my mother took it in stride. I can only guess she loved him and he made her feel more secure.

WE ARE OUR MOTHERS' DAUGHTERS

A couple years passed and Patricia became pregnant with my older brother Andrew. During that time she wrote her first novel. She completed most of it before her seventh month. She took two months off work before Andrew was born and completed the book during that time. Patricia was told by publishers to whom she submitted the work that the story was too sensational and scandalous to be taken seriously, although the story was based on actual events. Her first novel would never be published.

Two years later in 1963 I was born. In that time, my dad got sick and he was emotionally and mentally ill. He went into a hospital for a while. He visited a psychiatrist once a week as long as I can remember and still was extremely sensitive and obsessive and yelled a lot. Since this is my mother's story, I will not detail this here, but I know this was very challenging for my mother. She continued to work and take care of our home.

Mother got a job at Boise College (eventually this became Boise State University) as a secretary and worked there for almost 20 years. Even though she had summers and Christmas seasons off as the offices were closed, she still took classes in the summer. I remember that she took a class in ESP once, and always music classes. She was left handed and when she took a conducting class, the teacher would not let her conduct left handed. He told her she had no musical ability whatsoever because she struggled conducting right handed. She was furious with him, but did not take his criticism too seriously. But as usual, I remember she was very dramatic in her expressions of frustration. She loved drama.

My mother was left handed and had brown eyes. The rest of us in our immediate family were right handed and had blue eyes. As a child, my rationale for her left handedness was that she had brown eyes. It made sense to me. She was never hindered by her left handedness nor did she express that there was anything unusual about it. I know she was never forced to use her right hand as a child. In the 1920's and 1930's society was far less tolerant of those NOT right handed. My grandparents embraced her uniqueness. Grandma taught her many things by sitting in front of her like a mirror using her right hand which was opposite Mom's left hand. Mom was always appreciative of the left handedness support.

54

My mother was constantly moving. She worked a full time job, she managed the money, paid the bills, did all the shopping, went to school, took classes, participated in little theater productions, served as the secretary for Our Lady Shrine, taught Sunday school and took care of the house and us. When I was 7 my mother got sick and was in the hospital for 2 weeks. By that time my sister had moved out so it was just my father, brother and me. My dad said that I was now responsible to do all the things my mother would do. I was expected to make dinner, clean the house, clean the three bathrooms, mop and vacuum the floors, do the laundry, change the sheets, iron the clothes …. I hated it and vowed never to be married to anyone who expected that of me. I was exhausted and furious that my dad and brother sat and did nothing. I began to see that my mother was taken advantage of terribly and thought that was why she got sick… I wanted to get sick too.

When my mother came home I never complained about helping with the chores; if I did it was to myself. I respected her more and was more perplexed than ever. She did not complain; she just did it. She was determined to do it all. We used to sing Helen Reddi's "I Am Woman" and laugh at the commercials, "I can bring home the bacon, fry it up in a pan, and never let you forget you're a man." She demonstrated the life of an independent liberated woman. I admired her and believed in her. But I also knew she was not liberated when she was still a slave to the multitude of expectations of men. I think for her life was always filled with work and it did not serve to complain about it. As a mother now, with a full time job, an active life, responsible for so very much, and a slave to my bank accounts and my to do lists, I am completely at a loss as to how she was able to accomplish so much and remain light hearted and willing. She was often very silly and always a character.

My social skills and ability to make and be with friends was severely hindered by the obsessive compulsive environment in which we lived. My brother was also handicapped in the same way. But I could communicate with my mother. I told her everything (or so I thought – my daughter tells me things I would never have shared with my mom or anyone). When I was 12, my mother was my best friend. I remember every Wednesday evening we went to choir practice. Every

Sunday morning, we went to church. We would come home., set the roast cooking, then go for a bike ride. When we got home from our ride, we would play cards until the roast was done, serve dinner to the boys, clean up the kitchen, and then play cards until bedtime. This is one of the best memories I have of time spent with my mother.

During the balance of my childhood years, my mother continued to work and go to school. She said she would graduate from college before I did or at the same time. Although that did not happen, I did attend college where she worked and I would visit her at her office.

My mother was also very psychic. She could see things no one else could and sensed things no one else sensed. My brother was not one to manage his time well and was often late for school. One time she came home and related to my brother exactly what had occurred after she and my father had left for work. She told how he had frantically dashed through the house, forgot his coat and dashed back in to grab it, missed the bus, and had to walk to school. In that moment my brother was horrified and intentionally blocked her out, pushed her out of his head. She could never read him again.

When I was in my 20's, I was in a car accident that left my car totaled and me with a head injury. My mother said she saw it, but she thought it was a vision of her in the accident. She rejected the vision immediately saying, "I don't have time for an accident – I have too much to do. NO!"

My mother liked loud, gregarious, and bright multi-colored stimulus. When I was younger she wore what she called her coat of many colors – named after the Bible story of Joseph. Later, she wore a bright red coat and a red turbine on her head. Once I remember that she was at work and was instructed by some presence to walk across campus in her bright red coat. She did as she felt prompted and made the hike past the elementary school on campus and ventured into an empty building (the college kids and classes had gone home for the Christmas season, but the elementary school was still in session). There she asked the presence, "What am I doing here?" She felt prompted to buy a candy bar. "I don't have any money." She was prompted to reach in her pocket and found an exact amount of change and plunked it in the vending machine. Without thinking, she pushed a button and a bright red candy bar dropped out. She picked it up and then proceeded to walk back to her office. She saw a strange man hanging out near the school yard, and he turned and walked away. She went back to her office and continued her work day. My mother was convinced that it was her walking by very visibly and walking back very visibly that made the man walk away.

My mother would talk about how she was drawn to certain people, and how she would have psychic connections with people. No topic that had to do with altered states of awareness was off limits.

The second novel my mother wrote was about a girl who was having an out-of-body experience and witnessed a murder. I remember she went to the research center in California when I was a teenager, The Monroe Institute, to do research for this book. Years later she admitted to me she considered staying there and not coming back to Boise. Without the limitations of obligation at home, she felt free and wanted to maintain that freedom. But she chose to make the journey back home, finish the book and seek publication. This was her second full-length novel and though she was never able to get it published either, she found a great deal of freedom in the process.

A few years later in 1981, my father died. My mother said that he finally set her free; that he set all of us free. For the remainder of her years before she retired, my mother struggled financially. My father's social security did not provide much support. He had a small pension that had been put in a retirement fund that she could not access until she was 59 ½. She was 54 when he died with two kids still at home. I was 17 and got a big chunk of money from social security and I believed it was my ticket out. I moved out of the house a few months after he died. My brother stayed on at home, but was lost and unsure of what to do with his life.

I struggled too, moving in with a very abusive boy, and struggling just to have food to eat. I was going to college but was very mal-nourished and when I would visit my mother at her office, she would always unpretentiously offer me half her sandwich because she knew I had not eaten. I took no thought of how this sudden move had hurt my mother because I, like her, was fiercely independent and determined to make it on my own. I was glad to be rid of the drama of my childhood. I just jumped into a different drama. Ultimately, this boy would beat me, and lie to me and threaten my life and then threaten my mother's and brother's life. I had a restraining order put on him and moved home for a little while, but then moved out again into my own apartment soon after.

I was very broke but independent. I knew my mother was pretty broke too, and I honestly did not remember but apparently she gave me money for food and rent. We talked about it years later and I still did not remember. Eventually, I got a great job learning to take photographs and sell them and it involved a lot of travel. It was a lifesaver for me. But I did not have a car and I could not have the job if I did not have a car. My mother cosigned on the loan so I could to buy a car. She had impeccable credit because no matter how broke she was, she always paid her bills. I ended up giving up my apartment since I was on the road most of the time and moved back in with my mother to help her financially.

This was the beginning of an important chapter in her life. It was early in 1984 and my mother was 57. She could not access the money my father had invested until she was 59 ½ so my moving in with her was the answer to her prayers. She had started giving private piano lessons to earn some extra money.

And then out of the blue her boss at the University brought in a computer for word processing but refused to give her any training on it. He said she was too old to learn it and she was due to retire anyway. My mother took it up with the school administration calling it age discrimination. Meanwhile, she helped herself to that computer. She was determined to learn how to use it. She went in to the office on the weekend, turned it on and just started playing with it. She picked it up pretty quick. Before too long, she was operating it every day and won the discrimination suit she filed against her boss. Years later, she surpassed many on the computer using sophisticated programs to write and print music. The standing joke is that she wouldn't take it sitting down, so she sat down to learn it!

That was my mother. She determined to do something and she did it. This is the reasoning I find when I search my own self, how did she have time to do the things she did? How did she have the courage to get off that train in Boise – alone with a baby? How did she make it work? How did she keep her house clean all the time, and do all the things to make us a home? She was determined. And that determination gave her the strength, courage and fortitude to persevere in the face of dramatic limitations.

Even though I was helping with the mortgage and the utilities my mother still struggled financially. I had learned from her the ways to stretch a dollar. And I was building my savings and paying for my car and insurance. I was appalled to discover that she was actually making less money than I was per hour at a job she had been in for almost 20 years and I was just barely 20 without a college education.

She continued to give private piano lessons and look for paying gigs to play her music. She did many weddings, funerals, and evening events for restaurant or other venue openings. I remember coming home one time off the road (my time off was usually two to three weeks at a stretch) and she was just a mess. She was crying because she had just had her piano tuned and the tuner had told her that the piano was wearing out and in need of repair. She was devastated and as with everything important in her life very dramatic. "What would she do?" "Was it hopeless?"

Now for a funny story that you can't tell anyone: In my travels on the road, I often had riders; other photographers, trainees, sales people etc. Well, the day I came home to my mother's tears, I cleaned my car after weeks on the road. As I pulled the seat back to pick up the inevitable trash and scraps of things that had gathered, I found a pipe. Hmmmmmm? What is this? I thought about who, among my various riders, might have left it in my car? I examined it carefully and found that it was not just a pipe. It had a hidden compartment. In that compartment was some serious marijuana with some serious red buds. Whoever had left it in my car had spared no expense. And I was helpless to know how to return it. I had just been in attendance at a fall work seminar in Oregon, so as groups of employees, we had traveled to restaurants and other places.

So, my mother and I were both adults with an adult relationship at this point. I was no longer the preteen child looking for my mother's advice or fearful of potential punishment, but rather we were peers, both struggling to make ends meet and searching for life's answers together. I showed her the pipe; showed her the marijuana, and told her my dilemma. Her response was to say, "Let's smoke it!"

WE ARE OUR MOTHERS' DAUGHTERS

I laughed because I knew she was serious. I had chosen not to smoke marijuana as an adult although I had tried it when I was younger and after I moved away from home. I limited my alcohol consumption too as I was terrified of doing something to put my job at risk. But here it was, and here we were, with this beautiful pipe, with the really good marijuana. I just hoped it was not laced with something else. So, smoke it we did.

My mother and I had also recently discovered the Unity Church. Unity was in line with so many of the beliefs we shared and was very accepting of the ESP, altered states of awareness, out of body experiences, and transcendental meditation that was emerging into our culture in the early 1980's. We had shared books and visioning boards, I was reading Leo Buscalia, Parmahansa Yogananda, Norman Vincent Peele, and all nature of self-help and spiritual books teaching us how to manifest our highest and best lives.

So here we were, two spiritually minded women, bent on learning about the psyche and how we make and picture our own lives having ourselves a smoke of marijuana in the kitchen, chatting away about our lives and my mom's dilemma over the piano. We laughed and danced, and let the day take us away. Then a strange thing happened. We began to vision Mom with a grand piano. We looked around and figured out where she would put it when she got it. She knew she could not afford it, but we were high. So since we were visioning we were visioning big. By the end of the day, Mother said she was going to have two grand pianos and she would travel the world playing and performing. And we ended it with the classic visioning statement, "this or something better is coming to me now in totally satisfying and harmonious ways".

The next day, my mother, a determined woman in everything, went to her local music store where she had many friends and told them of her vision. She probably left the part about the marijuana out of the story. But I'm sure she was very animated and excited. She told everyone she just needed money for a down payment and then she would be able to get a loan. She did not really know how she would make the monthly payments, but within a very short time she knew which piano she wanted and how much it was going to cost.

By the time the Christmas season rolled around, it seemed she was going to be saving a long time just for the down payment. But she kept the vision. I asked her if she had told my Aunt Agnes (my dad's sister in New Jersey) who was considerably more financially stable than my mother. I suggested that telling her might inspire her to help. My mother would never ask outright for help from anyone. That was NOT her style. But she called Aunt Agnes and caught up with her and told her of her plans and her hope that all her saving would result in the down payment coming soon.

And then I made my own decision. I was going to give her a Christmas present. I left this note on the table for her before going back on road.

Dear Mom,

I finally found your Christmas present. It was not on a shelf in any store, it was in a corner of my heart. My gift to you is a return of faith, faith in the rightness of things and faith in you. Please accept this gift in total satisfaction and harmonious ways. I give you your down payment. Even minus $1,000 in my savings I will have enough to survive. And what I don't have will come. I can't think of a better way to spend the money.

I love you, and I know this is right.

Love Forever,
Jane

I placed the check on the table under the note and took off for my next job. I called her when I got to my destination and she was crying. She told me that Aunt Agnes had called her back that day and told her she was going to give her $1000 for a down payment. Now she not only had $1000 but $2000 to put down on the piano. The total price for the new Kawai 6'1" grand piano was just over $10,000. If I recall, she took delivery on it before Christmas.

The year was 1986 and Mother was nearing retirement age. She had continued to take classes at the University, teach piano (she had some really good students), take piano lessons herself from Madam Shu (who had been her teacher for years), then later Del Parkinson

61

would be her primary piano teacher. She would play in various venues and she continued to work at the university and was making her monthly payments on the piano.

I had had a very good year financially and had won the honor of top salesperson, most improved salesperson and some other award I cannot remember. Each award came with a trip and cash. I asked if I could combine the trips into one and was told yes. So Mother and I went to the World's Fair in Vancouver British Columbia Canada. One week we stayed at a fancy hotel in Downtown Vancouver, and another week we spent on a cruise ship (The Pegasus) docked in the harbor to accommodate the visitors from around the world. It was really awesome.

It was on the Pegasus and at that fair that my mother would find fuel for the fire burning inside her to be what she was meant to be. And this would be the beginning of the fulfillment of the second part of our visioning. She met a cruise director who encouraged her to make a demo tape (something she had never done, nor had it ever been suggested). "We are always looking for musicians and talent," he said. We had a wonderful trip, but of everything we saw, and everything we did, and the closeness we shared on that journey, this was the biggest takeaway.

She went home and immediately made a demo tape and started sending it out to cruise lines and resorts.

The next summer, my mother agreed to drive a friend's car down to the Grand Canyon and meet her there. She stayed for 3 months on the North Rim and worked in the lodge. She would play piano every night in the lounge and work in the store in the day. She proclaimed that she had "never worked so hard, for so little money, and had so much fun in all her life". What a statement.

She retired in 1988 at 62, but it was then that she came alive. She had her plans made and had been booked on a few cruises. She went to Alaska and Hawaii on cruise ships and was paid to do it. She continued to go to school and traveled with the Boise State Music Department to New York and London several times. She finally got her Bachelor's degree in Music Fine Arts in 1992.

But for her the quest for education was more than a degree; it was an opportunity to make her life's play a story of triumph. She wanted to be the next Grandma Moses. She continued her education and got a second Bachelor's degree in Theater. In this program, in 1995 at the age of 68 she studied as a French Exchange Student in Pau France and lived there for 3 months. Her stamina was amazing to me and to all who knew her.

In 1997, I was living in North Carolina, and Mother wanted to come visit us, but on the way she wanted to see the ruins of Machu Picchu Peru. The plan

was she would fly from Peru to North Carolina for Christmas with us. But then suddenly, she found herself in a hospital bed. She had been sporting a sore jaw whenever she rode her bike. So one day she rode her bike to the hospital. They would not let her leave. She was having a heart attack. And the solution was surgery (stints) to keep her from dying. On the way to surgery, she gave my Aunt Kay (Mother's sister) the cash and the directions for the travel agent. It was September and she wanted to get the tickets right then because the price was right. When I heard of this, and then found out that my Aunt actually went ahead with the purchase, I was furious. Aunt Kay told me she was

WE ARE OUR MOTHERS' DAUGHTERS

NOT going to argue with my mother. My mother was after all a force to be reckoned with and I understood.

The doctor and everyone thought she was crazy. But 12 weeks later – the doctor declared her fit to travel. She went to Peru but did not hike into the ruins as it was too strenuous. She flew on to North Carolina and was with us for that Christmas.

In the years that followed, my brother died and Mother had to carry on. Carry on she did. She continued to travel and write and she loved to read mystery novels. She would become a grandmother twice more. Mother would take a couple more cruises and travel to Europe again. My mother's answering machine stated in her sing song silly way was thus, "Life is so exciting and I'm having so much fun that you'll have to leave a message, 'cause I'm always on the run!"

Mother would travel to her hometown in Flandreau South Dakota a few times as well and it was to there that she would take her last trip. It was also very fitting. It was 2002 and the 4th of July. A celebration and homecoming was organized to honor the fallen American Heroes of that area. Her brother Bill was among the fallen. She traveled with her sister Kay. When she got home on the 7th, we had a grand phone conversation. She went on and on about whom she had seen, what she had done, how things had changed. She went to the old house and store where she grew up and overall was blissfully happy. It was kind of cool. I knew this had been an important journey for her. I felt compelled in that conversation to just listen and be in that bliss with her. I knew I would catch up with her later and she was scheduled to arrive in Kansas City where we were living in just a week. I had just been given a piano and was excited to show it to her.

Later that evening, I sat down and composed a tune on the piano. It came so easily and it was beautiful. With ease I filled in the tune with chords and runs and character. It is the only piece that I have ever written that to this day I can sit down and play without errors.

It turns out that was the last conversation my mother and I would have on this level of existence. We think it was shortly after that conversation she had a stroke and passed out on her bed. I believe she was in communication with me through the song that poured out of me at the piano. A neighbor found her three days later in a coma. She was taken to the hospital and died the next day. I was not there, nor was my sister, but she was surrounded by friends.

I found the note I had left her giving her the down payment in the piano bench when we came to her house after she died. She had also specified in her will that the grand piano was to go to me. I had the piano shipped directly to a music company in Kansas City to have it cleaned and give it any needed repairs. The piano man (also the name of the company) told me that every key was worn down equally and he recommended new pads. He said normally only the middle keys are worn down. My mother had never gotten the second grand piano we had envisioned that day, but she had played every key on that piano, traveled the world, and made the most of that wonderful vision, and made the most of her life.

Wherever she went, whatever group she was a part of, they became her family. That was her way. That is the legacy she left me with. Wherever she went she was putting on a show and everybody was rooting for her; her determination was an inspiration to everyone she knew.

And at the time of her death she was in the process of completing her master's degree in musical theater. To accomplish this, she first had to convince the university to create such a degree as they did not have one. She only had a small amount to do to complete the degree and one of her theater friends took to task to get the final work submitted to the committee in charge. The University gave her that degree posthumously.

65

WE ARE OUR MOTHERS' DAUGHTERS

The letter we received from the university accompanying her Master's Certificate said it all.

> *"... your mother ... was always, despite her maturity, one of the most energetic and enthusiastic theatre majors. She loved musical theatre more than anyone (we) have ever known...*

> *Your mother defended her graduate thesis project in the spring of 2002. Her graduate committee (was) most impressed with the progress of her work. We were struck by her sheer tenacity and enjoyment of the rigors of the academic process. We were also very much in awe of her determination to finish this degree, a task to which she devoted much time and hard work...*

> *I can promise you that we will never forget her and that we will continue to miss her deeply. We will also continue to be inspired by her strength and her sheer love for the theatre."*

This letter was signed by the Chair of the Theatre Arts Department at Boise State University, Dr. Richard Klautsch and represented the shared sentiment of Dr. Del Parkinson and Prof. Wally Bratt, her graduate committee. My sister and I stand in gratitude to all the people who made the posthumous award to her master's degree possible including the multitude of friends she had in the local theater community.

Patricia Durie's last show was perhaps a quiet bow into death. But her funeral would be her final curtain call where the multitude of people whom she had loved and loved well came to applaud and celebrate her. And her master's degree was the final bow. Patricia Durie's life was a life well lived, a complete life; with loud and purposeful mistakes and triumphs, well developed characters and story lines, well written with a triumphant ending. How we loved her and how sad we were to see the final curtain go down.

Janie Frederick is the daughter of Patricia J. Durie and the author of this essay. Like her mother she is tenaciously committed to whatever is in front of her and cannot leave anything unfinished. She has carried on the artistic traditions of her parents. Janie has done acting and singing on stage and like Patricia is an author (from a very young age) of poetry, short stories and music.

In the family tradition, Janie has been in school a large portion of her adult life. Janie went to college for a year after graduating from high school in 1982 but then left college to take a job traveling 35,000 miles a year doing portrait photography. She went back to school for a year in Oregon before she moved to Kansas City, Missouri, in 1990 where she met her husband of 26 years. She finally completed her liberal arts degree in 1994 then went on to seminary to complete a degree in ministry in 1997. She was ordained in 1997.

Then in 2003, while raising her two children, Janie went back to school to get her bachelor of science in accounting. She graduated in 2005 and later got her CPA credentials. Although she feels very educated, Janie has never considered her education complete. She currently lives in Kansas City, Missouri.

"The people I come from are passionate artisans with a great appreciation for beauty and education. This has made me who I am. I care deeply about the world and its people and I want the beauty to remain long after I am gone. I hope that like my mother, I can inspire and motivate people to be their best; to never give up and always make the most of the life they have been given. I hope to instill the values in my children she instilled in me and that when I leave the planet, I have given as much to the world as she did. I am my mother's daughter and I miss her every day."

4

Live a BIG Life

MARY ANN CZLAPINSKI

1937	—	2001
Montague City, Massachusetts		New Britain, Connecticut

By Victoria Jas

The phone rang, early enough to be foreboding… causing one to jump out the depths of sleep, and ask, disoriented, is the whole family safe and asleep in their beds? My mother was up, quietly dressing in the dark, tea kettle already on the stove, to fill the travel thermos. She

Mary and Ed, 1990

stood close to the stove, so she could lift the heavy kettle before the whistle woke the rest of the house. Lipton tea, always Lipton tea, with a splash of milk. My seven-year-old self rolled out of bed, recognizing an opportunity for an adventure with my mother into the dark, too little to understand any other reason for a call so late into the night. I wandered downstairs and asked the question I would always ask, still ask, "Can I go too?" This time, the answer was no, but eventually I was thought to be old enough.

In the days before the internet, the telephone tree announced an opportunity for my mother to exercise her obsession of bird watching. This time it was a life bird (a bird, if you were lucky, you might see once in your lifetime), a Great Grey Owl, who should have been happily catching rodents in northern Canada, but instead was seen at pre dawn at a backyard bird feeder by a bird watcher good enough and respected enough to elicit a private invitation by phone to come and see the bird. Hundreds of people would come in the next few hours on a February morning, from all over New England. It would be a mass pilgrimage, a sacred meeting of a very large wild creature who was far from home. All on a Monday morning, many of the disciples being late to work by the time they returned home, much satisfied nonetheless, with a little wildness still lofting about their day.

My mother inspired a life-long love of nature in me, and I still feel the excitement of the adventure, of what I might see, hear or feel when I am outside. I still keep a thermos near the tea kettle, and my mother's life list (of birds observed) is close to my bed, along with my library of two generations of guidebooks. She was with me in spirit when I drove around for hours trying to find the already-alerted Snowy Owl near my house a few years ago. It was a combination of a quart of hot tea, my mother's bird book for luck, and perseverance that I finally saw the lovely owl, sitting on the ground, looking a bit confused that it was not on the arctic tundra, but in Springfield, Vermont, by a trailer park. I was thrilled.

My mother, Mary Ann Czlapinski, was born Mary Ann Sharp, on June 6, 1937, on a hill farm in Montague City, Massachusetts. She had an older sister Rudy and brother Robert, with another twin sister and brother who passed in infancy. Her parents barely made ends meet. The Depression forced them to leave the farm and move to central Connecticut where they hoped that they could operate another farm and have a better life. They were able to start a small farm, specializing in flowers, then expanded by army contracts to grow food for the troops. During World War II, there was enough money to heat the greenhouses, or the family home, but not both: all daytime activities, including homework, were done in the greenhouses among the warm plants. They were scrappy people who knew how to fix anything, grow and preserve their own food, and not ask anyone for help. They were proud but also insular, so accustomed to working hard together that they were uncomfortable with idle time with strangers.

My mother had a childhood where there was little time for play, but a lot of time spent working outdoors. Her mother Marion encouraged an appreciation of and curiosity for the natural world. Schooling ended at fifth grade when Marion died of breast cancer in 1950. My mother went to work in the greenhouses on a full time basis, with the business later returning to growing flowers, and later creating a flower shop *Flowers by Sharp*, in Plainville, Connecticut, with Rudy.

71

Both sisters married. Rudy had a son, Michael, in 1954, then Mary a son as well, my brother, Tim, in 1957. I was born in 1962, with my sister, Laurel, in 1964.

My mother was not formally educated. She never became famous. Mary rarely gave me advice. She would definitely be bewildered by the tiger moms of today, pushing their children about like little pawns in some bizarre global chess game. She grew up in a world without after-school activities, sports, music lessons, and summer vacations. I often wondered while growing up if the loss of her mother when Mary was only 13 so altered her perspective, causing her to avoid advice, as she had received none in her formative years; not seek it as a young adult, and certainly not to give it as a parent. She felt alone because she was alone, and keeping her own counsel was not a choice. She found her own way.

Asking my mother for advice was like asking Buddha how to fix a car. She would only convey her confidence that I would figure it out, leaving me, first as an adolescent, with the idea that she truly was entirely out of touch; later when I became a parent, I would eventually create my own interpretation of this hands-off approach. Her confidence inspired me to be the first in my family to graduate from

high school. She passed her GRE– at 43 years old- along with her second husband the year after I finished high school. Her gift to me was her faith in hard work, and the confidence that I could achieve whatever I was willing to sacrifice for and commit to. Her obstacles of poverty, a lack of an education and an abusive first marriage to an alcoholic would not become mine, not if she could help it. I asked her once if her confidence in me sprang from the knowledge that I had more

Mary, Age 8, 1945

resources than she did in her childhood. She looked surprised and disagreed. I told her that I always knew that she had my back and material things were helpful but not as necessary to nurture and love me. She gave me what she was not given. She created where there was a void. So while she may have been confident in me, I was in awe of her. This was in stark comparison to my father, who as a volatile alcoholic.

My father disappeared for long periods of time, when we were very young, and became a stranger to us. He was physically abusive when sober, and a jolly drunk. Most of his 12 siblings counseled my mother to let him be drunk all of the time as he was more tolerable. I can remember being forced to

Mary and her father, 1949

watch my father beat my brother, with our father explaining to us that girls shouldn't be physically hurt. That was supposed to be a parenting lesson in his twisted mind. Hit boys! It toughens them up, but don't hit girls, because we are supposed to be weak, needing protection and dominance. It was okay in his world to torture young female (read subservient) minds. I was probably 5 and these are some of my first memories as a child. At that point, my mother didn't need advice, didn't give advice. She lived and taught by example and was one of the bravest survivors that I have ever met. She stood up to him and would not allow him to hurt her children. She told him to leave, despite having no income of her own, despite knowing that his Polish Catholic family would disown her and her children. Mother's own father had passed away when she was 18. She had no man to protect her against her own husband. Restraining orders were not in existence to protect against domestic violence and women were just expected to put up with the lives over which they had little control.

WE ARE OUR MOTHERS' DAUGHTERS

My mother stood up for us by making a decision that was taboo in the 1960's: you simply did not leave a marriage, for any reason. But she did. Little did she know that a year later, she would be diagnosed with tuberculosis, forced into quarantine in a sanatorium, and her children would be taken away. We were poor, separated from each other and our mother was seriously ill. I don't usually share these family memories with anyone because I want strangers to form their own opinion of me first: me now, not my past. Knowing my graceful, quiet, bird-watching mother, one would never guess the bravery and strength of character that lay beneath. I would not have the strength and resiliency that I have today had I grown up in another household. I later learned to quell the desire to make up a new history of my early life so that I could fit in with 'normal' people.

My family spent a year apart with Mother in a sanatorium, sleeping on porches in the fresh air, in quarantine during a time when treatment for TB was still in development. Tim, Laurel and I went into three separate foster-care homes and we had no idea when or if we would ever see our mother or each other again. She recovered, and we were returned to her, but our father was gone, officially missing until claimed legally dead.

We moved into public housing and received public assistance as Mother got back on her feet. Life went on. No grieving for the lost father was allowed. The story was that "everyone" was glad to see him go, and the adults secretly hoped that he would not return. Our questions about this were not answered. It was so awful and unknowable that it was ignored. My mother feared his return for years. To this day we do not know what happened to him.

A family of four people meant that my mother had to support us, and she began to sell Avon products out of her car, with three children riding along for hours during deliveries as she had no money for a babysitter. She had no sales background, but she found it easy to speak with other women and she was a hard worker. Jobs such as being an "Avon lady" were early routes for women in creating jobs that could co-exist with their parenting responsibilities, which was a fairly new concept. She often worked a few jobs at a time. I was in charge of my sister, who was always medically fragile. We learned to be self-sufficient and that no one had the right to hurt us. We learned very early on to stand up for ourselves.

This strength is now called grit, or resilience. It is forged through experiences that required you to carry the load yourself, and for others at the same time, when the adults should be doing this for you. It must have broken my mother's heart that her children had to go through a similar experience as she had, and as much as she tried, that she could only do so much to improve all of our lives.

Hard work was indeed the way out of poverty, and she was able to slowly improve our economic situation. We went camping in a very smelly and primitive canvas tent so that we could get away from the housing project, which I remember as clinical and new. We moved forward in a healthier and less stressful environment. Mother knew the names of all of the plants, trees and birds, and she knew the location and hours of every free admission day for art or science museums in the state, and we went to them with regularity. We didn't own a radio or television, and the outdoors was our only entertainment, classroom and time to learn about the bigger world. I think getting outdoors kept her sanity intact under the constant strain of raising three kids, working, and getting her strength back after a year of TB treatment.

We lived on the second floor in this housing project. The single man who lived on the first floor was a car mechanic. One day, my mother's car died, and she was desperate for help. She remembered that this neighbor was a mechanic and put aside her pride and shyness and asked him for help. He rescued her car, she got to work, and all was well. He was a divorced dad of two children who lived with their mother. Help turned into friendship, then a more serious relationship and the two eventually married in 1967 with their combined five children at their side. They were both children of farmers during the Depression. Ed's family was a Catholic family with 12 children living on a dairy farm in Middletown, Connecticut. He had grown up in a family where only half of the children could attend church each week, because there were not enough shoes for everyone, and they were too proud to have other people know that (although during the Depression, this was the case for a lot of people).

Both areas where my parents farmed with their families were developed into housing or shopping malls after World War II. Ed liked being outdoors as well, and they would go out for walks together on the rare occasion when they were not working. Their hard work allowed them to purchase a house in the suburbs for $16,000. They paid off their mortgage as fast as they could, had no debt, only made purchases when they had cash, and got their first credit card after retirement so that they could drive to the Yukon in their old truck, camping along the way. They were equally frugal and proud of being so. The household trash was examined weekly before going out to the curb, in search of something that could be reused. Between the two of them, they could make or fix just about anything. This only embarrassed me when I became old enough to understand that most of my friends had new school clothes, while mine were made at home, or were hand-me-downs from my brother. I was lucky that I was a tomboy and preferred flannel shirts anyway, but it was tough on my rather lady-like sister. My parents had found love, companionship and security for all of us, all more important than new clothes.

Vikki and Mary, 1994

Mother and Ed eventually joined an Audubon group of fellow birdwatchers, and would go out on weekends or sometimes during the weeknight (we called that "whooping it up," because no one ever went out during the week) to attend a slideshow about a fellow member's trip to Guatemala. or some other exotic place. My mother had never left the United States until they drove across Canada to reach the Yukon. She never flew in a plane. And to this day, my 87-year-old step father, who has a 3rd grade education, has never used a computer. But, here they were, in the 1970's, among doctors and lawyers, discussing bird watching. Although it was a long time until my mother could take time off from work to attend local trips with the group, she memorized bird song at home by listening to vinyl recordings and would study the families of each common, accidental or migratory bird. She was driven to know them. She found satisfaction in being sought out for her knowledge by those who had impressive educations and professions.

Vikki with pinwheel amid the flowers

My parents were the ones who fixed the cars or sold the flowers to the professional folks. It gave them something to be proud of, and a community that they were welcomed in regardless of class or background. They had become respectable middle class suburbanites, all of their hard work paid off, and they could begin to enjoy a hobby, a luxury that they had never known in childhood. Mother found time to be our girl scout leader and sing in local hospitals. She enjoyed painting and her work appeared in many local juried shows.

77

WE ARE OUR MOTHERS' DAUGHTERS

My restless drive to be independent comes from the instability of my early childhood. My fierce loyalty to my own children and my husband of 32 years (so far) arises from my mother's passionate protection of her family. My curiosity about nature and art are her gifts to me. We were very close when I became an adult. We had lots of laughs. She loved dumb jokes and puns, songs from the 1930's and 40s, idiotic 70s British humor, and Willy Nelson (she even forgave him his marijuana arrests). She became more silly--hokey, as she called it (not to be confused with hockey) as she got older. We never had enough paddles or enough camping trips. We went on a paddle with my aunt Rudy once in cold weather and Mother packed the same ratty canvas bag with a thermos of hot water, cookies and teacups, but forgot the tea bags. We drank hot water in our canoe, and were happy for the time together. I can only hope that all people have the pleasure of a shared silly family story like this one for us, that could make us laugh so hard in remembering that day, decades after the experience. She took and gave great pleasure in simple things, even forgetting the tea bags. My aunt enjoyed that joke with me until she passed away last year.

My mother found a lump on her neck that rubbed on her turtleneck shirts. It was cancer, a lymphoma with a 5% chance of living 6 months. She laughed at the grim doctor who was charged with giving her the bad news. Mother explained to this young man that her children were not married and she was not yet a grandmother. By golly, cancer was not going to mess with that life plan. It was not denial, it was her strong will to survive, employed once again. She lived 17 more years, saw her children all marry that first year after her diagnosis. My brother's son, my sister's son, and my son and daughter were all born in the following years. My mother died in my arms at 63, on March 2, 2001.

I especially felt her presence when I received my doctorate in environmental studies in 2009. I still think of her every day, and she is with me when I am in the woods, and I know that her spirit has returned to nature where she was happiest. She travels in my veins, my heart and my soul. I have a strong moral compass because of her sacrifice and for that I am eternally grateful. I watch the birds on our behalf, the last one reporting in now that my aunt is also gone.

It is one of my few regrets about my life, so far, is that my children never got to know their grandmother. She would have been an amazing grandmother. Her own mother had died at 38, long before I was born, so I also grew up without a grandmother. I so wanted this experience for, well, both me and my kids. If my children choose not to have their own children, I will have to find some kid out there who needs to watch birds or look under logs for centipedes. I have faith that we will find each other.

In the bird watching community, like other hobbies or pastimes, there are people who prefer to experience their activity in a more extreme manner. Some birdwatchers maintain lists of what they have observed. They compare notes and have a running contest over whose list is most impressive.

But some of the extreme birdwatchers, who are generally independently wealthy, compete in what is called the Big Year.

For one year, they select a geographic area and seek out every bird species available to be seen.

This requires many hours in a plane, car or boat, hotels and expensive field guides, strange hours, convenience store food, and lots of patience. Some of the participants employ such unsporting strategies such as flushing birds after they are observed, so others will not be able to see a particular group of birds.

The number of observed birds can fluctuate because species change in range, are flown off course during migration, or are thrown off course in a storm.

The American Birding Association record is 763 species in the United States, and 6,042 species globally. My mother kept a list of her efforts and enjoyed comparing notes with people. She did not have the means to travel much, but she enjoyed the process of keeping records. I have never kept a list because I am never sure if I have actually seen a particular bird or my mother first brought it to my attention (I call this phenomena parenting birding).

While my mother never had a big year, she had a BIG life, as her kindness and strength affected many people around her and she left the world a better place than she found it. Her ashes are under a tree in a park. She organized the effort to save this park from development in the 1980s. The park workers had the hole ready for the tree that would be planted over Mary's ashes, and were waiting for their friend who had worked tirelessly to save the park for birds and people. She rests there, among the birds, right where she'd like to be, keeping an eye on things.

Victoria Jas has been committed to living and working in a manner that leaves the world in a better place than she found it. Her 10th birthday coincided with the first Earth Day: "I remember seeing the Connecticut River flowing in various colors as the mills dropped dye into the ecosystem, I can remember seeing the first return of Bald Eagles as they slowly recovered from DDT. I was raised by a mother and aunt who were strong environmentalists and naturalists, teaching me not only the names of the animals and plants around me, but their importance as well."

She has been fortunate to work in the environmental field for her adult life, so far. She holds a B.S., M.S. and a Ph.D. in the environmental sciences and studies fields. She currently teaches environmental science and natural history, and has had her own environmental consulting practice since 2009.

Victoria is a certified Hazardous Materials Manager, a national certification for those working in both the technical and pollution prevention fields.

Her favorite projects solve problems by eliminating the use of hazardous materials altogether, instead of just managing waste streams. Her passion lies in walking the forested landscape, protecting it and sharing its wonders with others.

She has lived in Vermont for 30 years with her husband, Tom Hartman, and their two young adult children.

WE ARE OUR MOTHERS' DAUGHTERS

5

You Are the Oldest and Must Set the Example

MARY JEFFERSON SPROUL GREEF
December 10, 1904　　—　　November 9, 1971
Taylor, Texas　　　　Waynesboro, Virginia

By Nancy Cramer

My mother, Mary Jefferson Sproul, was born December 10, 1904, in or near Thrall, Texas, a small country town, about 35 miles northeast of Austin. Her ancestors were from Oberkaufungen, Cassel, Germany. The first one to arrive in Texas was Frank (Franz) Nolte in 1832 after an eventful voyage. Family stories tell of him stopping first in England, then being shipwrecked on Galveston Island, Texas. With some of his last gold coins, he bought two oxen and a wagon. General Sam Houston gave him a land grant for hauling food for him. He had left Kassel, located in western Prussia, because

of political upheaval and extreme poverty. Franz was widowed several times and may have had as many as five wives. He died in Buckhorn, Austin County, Texas on November 14, 1873. Another adult, Frederick Nolte, believed to be Franz's son, came with him from Germany.

Franz's father, Carl, was a shoemaker and a soldier back in Germany. He and his wife, Anna Gundelace, had six children, but evidently Franz was the only one who immigrated. When Franz was 63, he had become a successful farmer. In 1860 his worth was listed as $5,000, a good sum in those days. He and his successive wives may have had as many as ten children, but the next one we know about is Frank Herman Nolte, born in 1856.

In 1877, he and Mary Virginia Floyd of nearby Bellville were married. She was the grandmother of my mother, and possibly dearly loved from the number of photographs we have of her. Called "Mollie," a common nickname for Mary, she was probably the source of my mother's first name. My mother disliked the name and used to say, "Mary means sorrow and I don't like that."

Mollie and Frank Herman also had a big family of eight children, four girls and four boys. Two of the boys were in the army in World War I. One of them, Frank Alonzo, called "Lonnie," (too many Franks) was injured by mustard gas in the trenches in France. After the war, he married the school teacher who had been boarding with his family while he was gone. The Noltes evidently were a close family, as my mother talked about the times she spent at the farms of Uncle Boss or Uncle Murrah. One of my grandmother's sisters, Daisy Elizabeth Nolte, lived with my mother's family for many years until her marriage in 1927 to James McLean of Concordia, Kansas.

Somewhere among the line of children's names, the name "Jefferson," crept in. Possibly honoring the third U.S. President, Thomas Jefferson, one son from another branch of the family, the Floyds, was christened "Jefferson." Thus the appendage in my mother's name. The Floyds were the family of Grandmother Mollie of English ancestry. There was another Carl Nolte who is supposed to have fought in the Civil War. Probably he was named after the first Carl Nolte, the ancestor in Germany. He lived from 1776 to 1849 and perpetuated this particular line of Noltes.

Frank Harmon Nolte was born in 1922, most likely a grandson. He married and had ten children. One of his sons was Clarence F. Nolte, who also farmed, then later became a railroad inspector. There was a strike against the Santa Fe Railroad, after which he became a carpenter. Perhaps the strikers were fired.

Family lore has the story that a group of people from what was Prussia in Germany, brought with them all the tradesmen and officials, including minister, to replicate the village they had left behind in Germany. This would have been in the early 1800's. The evidence for this is scarce, but it is interesting to contemplate.

The earliest photo we have of these ancestors is of another Frank Herman Nolte, born August 25, 1856. He is leaning against the porch edge of the Nolte farmhouse. With his unshaven beard, uncombed hair, and rumpled and soiled suit, he looks like a fellow "no one would want to mess with." Not that he is large and tall, but his stern look and large nose makes one uneasy when viewing him. The farm was in cotton country, but as far as I know, they hired no blacks to do the backbreaking job of picking cotton. Of course, by then, it was illegal to own slaves, but many farmers hired them at "pickin" time. The house looks more like a rough slab cabin than a house. It is unpainted and crudely built.

An earlier photo of Frank Herman, not dated, shows him as a toddler with Grandma Mary Floyd Nolte (Mollie) and a young relative, Claudia, amidst a cotton field. The elderly appearing Grandma Nolte, is holding young Frank on her right side and Claudia on her left side. The cotton is as tall as the children are and Grandma is kneeling or squatting with barely her face showing among the cotton plants. Cotton was king in those days, and the vast field behind and around them must have required a lot of labor.

Another photo of an elegant house, belonging to Uncle Boss, probably located in nearby Taylor, has two stories with a captain's deck on top. Each side has windows on the second floor, and there is the typical southern wrap-around front porch. A round tower structure stands at each corner of the front porch. A Grecian style arch crowns the front door. The house and large yard are surrounded by a white painted picket fence with pointed pickets alternating in height. It must have been quite an installation to size the pickets for that long a fence.

85

WE ARE OUR MOTHERS' DAUGHTERS

A windmill in the backyard and two electricity poles complete with glass insulators fill the left side of the photo. A church, several blocks distant, to the right in the photo, has a tall wooden steeple Lutheran style and is two stories tall also. Several tiny figures stand on the church porch, perhaps several men and two children. They are barely visible due to the distance of the church and the large fence surrounding the building.

One album contains many poses of my mother beginning from infancy to girlhood. In one photo, she has short bobbed hair with a huge bow on the left side of her head. She is dressed in a lovely lace and ruffled white dress, wearing a tiny locket on a chain. She sits in an old style wicker chair. Her father, William Clarence Sproul, or "Bampa" as we called our grandfather, was a professional photographer, and she evidently loved to pose for him. I surmise that from the number of photos that have been preserved. Her face is slightly lit up and her head is framed in light. She definitely has an angelic look, solemn as always but with an inner sweetness.

In another portrait of her with her baby brother, Maurice or "Morrie," she is probably about five and he is just over one year in age. She again wears the big hair bow and a white dress trimmed in lace, but not as fancy as the other one. Our grandmother sewed beautifully, and my mother's dresses are probably the products of hours of "Bommie's" needle and thread. The photo is oval shaped. My uncle is wearing a dress, white socks and what looks like black leather sandal type shoes. They seem to be two children of proud parents. However, I am puzzled why my mother never smiled in any photos, even those of her as an adult. Perhaps it was not the fashion. My sisters and I have concluded that our mother, especially in her later years, suffered from depression. But at this early age?

Another old photo printed on heavy card board shows her wearing a huge bonnet tied under her chin. She is sober looking again, and is dressed in a dress with pleats that start at the hipline. Black stockings and high laced up shoes complement the long sleeves with cuffs and a large lace trimmed collar. She is probably six or seven then. My mother told us of having had diphtheria about that age and losing most of her hair, due to a high fever. Bommie constructed a series of bonnets to conceal the hair loss, and in one photo, the bonnet is fancy enough to have been worn by a bride. Little squiggles of curls peer out from the sides to frame her face, while she clasps her hands demurely in front of her. These numerous photos duplicate this pose into her married years. They make me wish I could have been there to hear the directions of "Turn your head this way," or "Don't smile." "Sit still, we're almost finished."

My curiosity is aroused when I look at the fancy clothes my mother wears in all her photos, contrasted with the look of poverty of the Nolte family photos. Surely the photography business was not that profitable to afford such garments. Perhaps my grandmother took in sewing. I don't know. My grandfather had been born in Waterville, Kansas, where he grew up and learned photography, perhaps from a J.J. Sproul, who may have been his father or a brother. Waterville was at the end of the cattle trail from Texas. There the cowboys were paid after the long dusty

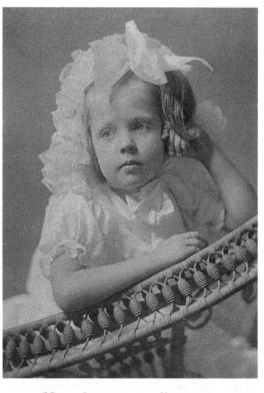

**Mary in an angelic pose
About age 4**

drive of 600 miles or so with hundreds of cattle. They had money to spend, and getting their picture taken, cleaned up and in new clothes, was a necessity, not a luxury. My great-grandfather also conducted the church choir, and we have a book presented to him by the choir as the inscription testifies to. Where he and his son, William Clarence, received their musical training is but one more of the mysteries of the Sproul family line.

However, the trail head changed to another site, and took the cowboys' dollars away from Waterville. As a result, in the late 1800's my great-grandfather moved his family to Texas. There his son, William Clarence, my grandfather, met and married my grandmother, Margaret Nolte Sproul, or "Maggie," as she was commonly called. I have been unable to trace the Sprouls back beyond my great-grandfather except that they came from Kentucky or thereabouts to Kansas.

As written earlier, Great Aunt Daisy Sproul, a single lady and sister of my grandfather, is listed in the 1910 Taylor city directory as a milliner, while my grandfather and his brother, Joseph, or J.J., are described as photographers.

About 20 years ago, my sister, Carol, and I visited Taylor, Thrall, and environs and were thrilled to find the house in Taylor where our mother grew up. We also found the buildings where the photography studio and millinery shop had been. The front of our mother's house faced sideways to the street. Had there been another narrow street that the house originally had faced? It is difficult to tell because the roads would have been dirt. Today they are paved and grassy lawns cover what might have been a street.

There are no pictures that survive of a school, or mention of one, except the high school in Canton, Ohio, from which my mother graduated. We have her huge diploma, beautifully framed in black and measuring at least 24"x30" from the early 1920s.

Back to our maiden Aunt Daisy. Though not the striking beauty that our Mother was, nevertheless Aunt Daisy had bountiful shiny, wavy, hair, piled up in a huge mound atop her head. Her tiny waist was accentuated by a narrow cloth belt, over a skirt and a full blouse topped with a high lacy collar. The dress was trimmed in rows of lace. She looks to be a young girl, perhaps 18 or 19. For some reason, she did not marry until late in life to James McLean, a Kansas farmer. How did they meet? Another mystery. They had no children. I have a box of romance books from the early 1900's she gave me, as well as some other books with more serious and classical contents.

An informal family photo made in 1911 or 1912 shows eleven people outside an unpainted clapboard house. The photo is labeled with names of the people. Most are Noltes. Some of them have clean faces and combed hair, others boast of their work stained clothes. My mother and Morrie and a huge black dog are among the children. Many names are familiar because of my hearing stories about them: Uncle Boss and Aunt Ida; Minnie and Murrah Nolte; Lonnie and old Grandma Molly. She is pictured by herself in another photo, wearing a nice dress, skirt reaching her ankles, complete with hose and pumps. In a picture quite unlike any others that survive, my mother, about 10 or 12, is seated in a buggy holding the reins of a well groomed horse. The caption says in my grandfather's handwriting, "Horse and Buggy Days." Again, my mother looks serious. Maybe driving the buggy wasn't her usual job. At some time she began to take piano lessons, possibly from my grandfather, who also tuned pianos. He claimed to have perfect pitch, which I witnessed while he worked on our piano. He did indeed identify correctly each note I played. It must have been an asset in his work, although tuning forks were available then, I am sure. Another question arises- how did he learn to tune pianos?

As an aside, my grandfather was a small, thin man, 5 foot 7 inches tall, according to his military record. He had a soft voice and gentle manner. He was kind in spirit and a good sport as illustrated by the tie I knitted for him when I was about 12 as a Christmas gift. It was alternating maroon and white stripes, and so much fun to "knit one, purl two," that I forgot to measure its length. He graciously wore it all day on Christmas, even though one end dragged on the floor.

There are scenes of picnics, not in a park, but in the countryside, usually near a river. I have two hand-tinted photos of a river winding through the countryside, with trees shading the shore line. Probably they are of the Brazos River near the family farms. The ladies are wearing sombrero type hats made of straw and are dressed fashionably, though probably uncomfortably, in skirts and shirtwaist with broad bands or belts. Texas can become very hot in the summer. They are seated on a log and appear to be holding sticks which doubled as fishing rods.

What do all these photographs say about what kind of a person my mother was? I was not sure. So I called to my surviving sister, Carol, who is 16 months my junior. (Our baby sister recently passed away at age 75 in very ill health.) One conclusion we arrived at was that our mother liked to be the center of attention. She was beautiful, well coifed, and stylishly dressed. She had a demure look at times; was coy in a few photos; and could be dramatic with her hair highlighted by studio lamps. Probably her father and later, her brother Morrie, also a photographer, practiced new ideas of posing and lighting on her. In one pose, she wears a wide band around her forehead, tied in back, with one long curl over a shoulder. She is younger, maybe 14 or 15, with an almost impish look. When her hands are depicted, they are delicately curved like a ballerina's and rest on her lap. Her dresses are always made of luxurious materials.

Mary with her brother, Morrie (left) and Nolte (right).

When she started being serious about playing the piano, we don't know. Nor are we aware of why the family moved to Canton, Ohio. I never heard of any relatives there. Perhaps there were friends or a job for my grandfather. He had joined the Texas State Militia some years previously. For another unknown reason, at some time after they moved to Ohio, he joined the Ohio National Guard, on Feb. 27, 1921, "serving in the second enlistment period at the time of his discharge." This was after the conclusion of World War I. His occupation was listed as a "grinder" and his health was "poor," so six months later, he was discharged October 25, 1921, for poor health. He was 45 years old and married, with three children by then. Perhaps times were hard and he needed to supplement his income with the tiny military pay. His character was marked in large letters as "Excellent."

In a letter to our mother, dated March 4, 1955, Bampa tells of his service in the Texas National Guard and also that he was an "employee of the U.S. Post Office Dept. in the capacity of mail carrier." Was that in Texas or Ohio? I need to do some research on this family. I also just recently discovered that two great-uncles served in World War I, and of course, George was in the army during the Civil War.

My mother graduated from McKinley High School in Canton, then went back to Texas, to Denton, where we later lived for 10 years, to attend Texas State College for Women. I don't know whose idea it was for her to become a teacher. Anyway, she had just one year in college, because most likely, finances created a problem. She went back to Canton, worked in a bank, and bought a baby grand piano for $450.00.

In sorting out boxes when my sister was here recently to help me celebrate my 85th birthday, we found all these photos and other treasures. We discovered an envelope full of receipts for her payments for the piano, $20 at a time. Sometimes they were monthly, sometimes skipping a month, depending upon, as the note from the bank says, the amount she earned by teaching piano students. So she worked two jobs, studied and practiced piano, and conducted a lively social life. At the time she met our father, probably 1928 or 1929, she was engaged to a "Tommy," who evidently was a well-to-do socialite, as I remember her saying.

91

WE ARE OUR MOTHERS' DAUGHTERS

But the handsome young man from Iowa, Charles Hill Greef, a graduate of Iowa State College with a degree in forestry in 1926, won her heart. They eloped to Clinton, Iowa, where they were married in a parsonage with two friends as witnesses. Mother had saved four or five clippings about the wedding announcements. One described Charles as "deserving popular during his high school days in Eldora and easily won for himself a position of influence and popularity during his student days in college. A member of the Alpha Tau Omega fraternity, he took a job with Curtis Woodwork, Inc. upon graduation." This lavish praise came, of course, from his hometown newspaper, the *Eldora Ledger.*

Mother's engagement and later wedding was also reported in the society section of the Canton newspaper. There were accounts of several showers and parties given for her as a new bride. One such party was a "bridge-tea" where the tables were decorated with sweet peas and ivory tapers. "The favors were French bouquets of sweet peas." Now, what are those? I am sure my mother loved every minute, as she liked a well-set table, good china and crystal, and of course, sterling silver flatware. She confided once that her father had remarked, "she had a champagne appetite on a beer pocketbook."

True, but she always managed to pay the bills somehow. I expect this attribute at times might have been a point of disagreement with my father, although he always dressed well and enjoyed parties and entertaining. But at heart, I think he held the basic Congregationalist views that his mother and Aunt Kate observed, keeping an eye to savings. This habit served my Grandmother Greef well during the Depression, because by then, Grandpa Greef was quite elderly and lost all his businesses in the drastic downturn of the economy. He had three lumberyards, many rental houses, and a plat of land in Eldora called the "Greef plat." All these and the vacant lots and unsold houses went to creditors. But my grandmother, true to her thrifty Scotch-Irish heritage, managed eventually, by the sales of lots and houses and rental collections, to repay every cent of her by-then-deceased-husband's debts. It took nearly ten years. We have copies of the deeds of sale to illustrate this.

To finish the descriptions of photographs from the early days of my mother to the time of her marriage, I must mention the several portraits of her with her two younger brothers. They were Maurice (whom you have already met) and Nolte, the youngest of the three Sproul offspring. None of the three siblings resemble each other. The size and shape of their eyes are different. Nolte has a dimple in his chin, and a calm appearance to his face. Morrie looks stern and determined, and my mother with her lovely folded hands, almost looks pleading. And none resembles either parent. Nonetheless, all evidently were well loved and looked after, and seemed to enjoy a good family relationship. So it seemed from copious letters, and the few long visits when we drove the long distance to Ohio from Texas. My mother and Morrie were especially close. She saved more than 100 of the letters he wrote, along with the tiny photos he took on a small camera when he served in China in the U.S. Air Corps. There's another book for me to write.

We rarely talked about serious matters. Her idea of Carol and me learning about the birds and bees was to take us to a female physician, who took out her medical book with its gruesome drawing of the female reproductive system. The male system was carefully shielded from our view, and as we had no brothers, our only knowledge of the male appendage was once when we were five or six and visiting friends. Then we accidentally had a glimpse. One of their sons, not aware of our presence, ran naked through the room on way to take a shower. I still remember his look of embarrassment today. The doctor's drawing was not any more helpful than a girlfriend's explanation: A girl is like a garage and the boy had a car to park in the garage. Naturally, we shared none of this with our mother.

This discussion and similar ones, including buying our first bras, evidently belonged in the category of "Just Not Discussed." Wearing the proper shoes with a certain dress fell under the topic of "It Must Be Done." My grandmother advised us to always wear hats and gloves when going to town, and of course, always change our underwear in case we fell down and hurt ourselves. Now the latter made sense, and I follow it today. As I have said, my parents were the products of their era. They had learned their lessons well, now it was our turn to be diligent students.

Carol and I concluded that we have to measure our mother's maternal instincts, not by what she said, but by what she did. We were always dressed nicely; in fact, we wore identical dresses until age 12. Carol was tall for her age, and we did look very much alike, so people often thought we were twins. I think our mother bought the same dresses so we wouldn't argue about whose was prettier. We admit that we quarrelled a lot, and Carol even claims "to have been a pain in Mother's backside." That's not the word she used, but you can figure it out. She and mother definitely clashed on just about everything. I think it was the second child birth order syndrome, Carol had to carve out her own identity. But, I was her first born. I remember my mother often saying: "Nancy, you are the oldest. You must set the example." So, I had no choice but to be the "goody goody," and always sought approval. While mother usually agreed with me, our father vigorously defended Carol, when was home on the weekends from his traveling sales job. When Gara was born nine years later, of course, being the baby, she was perfect. So it goes in families.

Once Carol committed some offense against me, (we neither can remember what it was), I threw a book at her. She ducked, and the book hit a window pane. Mother made her pay the 75 cents it cost for repairs, a punishment, as Carol claims "because she ducked instead of getting hit." I have felt bad about that incident for years and tried to repay her, but Carol just won't take my 75 cents, even with interest.

We often quarreled over whose turn it was to wash and whose turn it was to dry the dishes. No dishwashing machines then. Or when scrubbing the kitchen floor, and waxing with Johnson paste wax, then polishing it to make a shine, we argued who got the dirtier side. I have often wondered why our mother put up with all our squabbling. But justice prevailed when I had my own four children to assign to household chores. I never learned mother's secret. Maybe it was because I didn't have a room I could seek refuge in and close the door.

What she did for us was to expose us to all kinds of activities and learning. She sat in the scorching sun, shaded by a few trees, day after day by the pool while we learned to swim. She found a ballet teacher, and we practiced prancing around the house in graceful dips and jumps, until our father decided he'd had enough of those acrobatics. I took piano lessons at age six and progressed nicely through "March of the Wee Folk," until it came to a recital the summer I was in third grade. Presented on our teacher's front porch, the parents all sitting on chairs covering the lawn, it became my turn. I bravely marched up the steps and sat down to play the first chords. Then the second chords. Then- where were the next notes? I started over again, and failed. Once more I valiantly tried, then gave up nearly in tears. The audience kindly applauded, but that was the end of the lessons. A few years later, I practiced often and could play well enough to accompany Christmas songs and hymns.

My mother still practiced and played the lovely and difficult classical music she loved. In Amarillo, she obtained a position as accompanist at the local music conservatory, work that my father did not consider "a job." I continued my musical study by taking voice lessons, and I sang solos for years at various places. An unexpected luxury my mother gave me when I went away to college in Missouri was a lovely set of white calfskin luggage. We had moved to Amarillo in 1947, my senior year in high school. Carol and I adjusted well, because we had next door neighbor our age who introduced us socially to a set of friends. But our mother had to leave behind the large set of friends in Denton she had known for years. In Amarillo there was no one to introduce her socially, and whileI think she was willing to leave behind some of the bridge playing and luncheons, she sought some other avenue to use her time. Volunteering was not espoused as it is today, although she did help at Gara's school in the PTA. Our father was happy in his new stay-at-home managerial commission lumberman position. I am sure he had become weary of 20 years of traveling all week.

On the other hand, Carol and I wonder, if his staying home all week and expecting a good dinner each night, could have been one cause of their eventual divorce. In Denton, household help was affordable and my mother had a cook and parttime maid. Perhaps familiarity is not always so desirable to a married couple used to days without each other. In Denton also, mother had her flowers. She raised beautiful jasmine and gardenias. The latter she sold weekly to a local florist, taking them from their bowl of ice water in the refrigerator to his shop. She did this as long as they bloomed, which was months. She loved roses and had a small terrace built which divided the various families of roses. I remember a gorgeous orange-red rose which had a royal name like Princess Something.

Mary with her daughter, Nancy, about age 7-8.

In retrospect, and that is how we have to judge the past, our mother was a good parent. She put our well being and interests first, and wanted us to have the good things of life. These may have included things that had eluded her, such as lessons and college. She was beautiful, intelligent, and had a strong sense of values that we could use to guide our lives if we chose. She also proved she could be independent and self supporting, capable of filling a job usually held by a man in the license office in Virginia.

My mother and father were products of their time period, as was to be expected. Children should be seen and not heard. They should obey compliantly, and be dressed properly for the occasion. They were not to be petted or hugged or even kissed too often. That just was not done. I suppose I interpreted their lack of demonstrativeness, as a measure of their love for me. So, it was with joy years later, in rereading the letters of both parents, I found their expressions of love for me preserved on paper.

In addition to some formality in the family relationships, there also was underlying tension. I learned of its true nature when she wrote that they were getting a divorce.

Divorce was almost unheard of in those days, the early 1950's. My mother had had no work experience for 25 years and had a child of 10 to raise on her own, with no income other than alimony and child support. She sold her prized baby grand piano on which she had practiced for years with the aspiration at one time to become a concert pianist. I am sure that must have caused her a great deal of pain.

After the divorce, she loaded the little Ford car she had just won in a drawing at a local grocery store. She and my young sister moved to Columbia, Missouri where I was a student in the school of journalism. She wisely enrolled in secretarial classes, learning how to type, keep books, and take shorthand. She and my sister lived in a small apartment near the University with a spare bed for me to occupy. Living with them would have helped on finances, but I selfishly refused. I had worked in the journalism school library that summer and taken out a loan from my sorority so I could continue living in the sorority house. I had just been chosen to be Rush Chairman, the second highest position in the sorority. It was something I found great satisfaction and challenge in doing.

My mother was upset, but when my father offered to pay my house rent and other sorority expenses, it became a moot question. I tried to visit my mother and sister at least once a week or more, but we both had tight schedules. I felt guilty sometimes in wanting to live the sorority life, but that was part of going to college in those days. We had parties with the fraternities, and I had dates each night of the weekend. It was also where I met my future husband on a blind date at his fraternity located at what was called the University of Missouri School of Mines and Engineering in Rolla, Missouri. I was also selected for the Outstanding Senior Award my last year. My three years in the sorority served me well. I gained much needed self-confidence as I broke out of the shyness that came with being a year younger than my classmates. It also offered me leadership opportunities, where my skills as a "leader" were not interpreted as "being bossy," as my mother felt compelled to remind me when I quarreled with my sister.

I am confident that there were times my mother was quite lonely. She would retreat into a shell of privacy when she was not with other people. In looking back, I think my mother had experienced times of depression all her adult life. There was the long worrisome month my sister spent in the local hospital with osteomyelitis. I would borrow my mother's car and go see my sister. She, despite the pain of her disease and her confinement to a hospital bed, reveled in being spoiled by the nurses. I often wonder now how my mother had the fortitude to manage this new life she had chosen. Perhaps she had some new sense of freedom, despite her problems, that helped her through the difficulties. She never talked about it, and it didn't occur to me to ask. One of the hundreds of questions I now regret not asking.

After my graduation in 1952, I accepted a newspaper position in Waynesboro, Virginia, because my fiancé was ordered to duty at Ft. Belvoir, VA, on the first leg of his army career. My mother decided to move to Ohio and stay with her parents and a bachelor brother until opportunity came her way.

That opportunity brought her soon to Waynesboro, Virginia, and to the boarding house where I lived. I worked as society editor and general news reporting at the small town daily. She and my sister moved into the old fashioned Victorian house operated by Miss Julie. Every night we had dinner with about six to eight other boarders around a huge walnut table. The Negro maid cooked delicious southern food. We ate family style, and afterwards, sat outside on the long veranda that circled most of the house. I met a class of people I had never encountered before. There was George whose favorite saying was, "Well, if I don't toot my own horn, who will?" I found out years later that Miss Julie was addicted to drugs and the doctor who shared dinner each night with us, was her source of keeping her together in exchange for a nightly meal.

I saw my fiancé, John, almost every weekend when he drove down from Fort Belvoir. My mother thought the match was not suitable and tried to talk me out of our engagement. I simply never heard her arguments. I was so sure I had met the love of my life. It was so romantic, how we met and how we had seen each other at parties on the weekends in college. In retrospect, parties every weekend really don't make a good basis on which to form a marriage. I am sure she cried many tears when she heard John's announcement that late September weekend. He had just received orders to report in three days to Fort Leonard Wood, Missouri. We could get married in Maryland where there was no waiting period. I had already bought my wedding dress for a late spring wedding. The ceremony with all its trappings would have to be forgotten.

In the best spirit of motherhood, my mother loaned me her wedding ring for the ceremony. The wedding vows were exchanged in the parlor of the Methodist Church in Hagerstown, Md. The minister's wife dressed me. Again, I am sure my mother wept about a stranger being the one who fastened the long row of buttons on the back of my dress. John placed my mother's ring on my finger. I wonder now how much my mother cried that day, but I didn't think about it then. It was so romantic and adventurous. We barely made it to Fort Leonard Wood in the three days.

We rented a one room apartment in Rolla, which was about 30-40 miles from Fort Wood, and shared the bathroom and the kitchen. I don't recall how I spent the long days, because John left by dawn to report to the Fort. I wasn't lonely although I had no friends there. But being in love and newly married must have made up for it. We spent our last six weeks together living on the Fort in a rented 17-foot trailer. My father came to visit us just before Christmas. I have a picture of me cooking dinner in the trailer for the three of us. I do remember having to wait until payday once to buy a 3 cent stamp to mail a letter. Again, love cushioned the difficulties.

Well, my mother soon got a job in Waynesboro, which turned into a plum. She became the license agent for the county, selling all kinds of licenses. She quickly adapted to the job and loved it. She and my sister took an apartment to which I returned three months later. I decided to stay with them because my husband had just boarded a train that took him to Seattle, and then to Korea. I was one month pregnant.

The baby and I stayed there for 16 months until John returned. My mother adored the baby, and in true grandmotherly fashion, shared with me all the wisdom she had learned raising three girls. I worked for a surgeon as his secretary and operating nurse, until the week before I was due. He told me he was a surgeon, not an obstetrician, and it was time for me to resign. Sure enough, a few days later, early in the morning, I went into labor. My mother closed the office and nervously drove me over the 26 miles of mountains that separated Waynesboro from Charlottesville, where the doctor and hospital waited for me.

WE ARE OUR MOTHERS' DAUGHTERS

I recently came across a old photo of my mother lying in a lovely white bed holding me, a two or three day old infant. I wonder when she visited me the week I stayed in the hospital, if she remembered that photo of her cuddling me in her arms. The photo was probably made by my uncle, her brother, a professional photographer. Just one of the dozens, if not hundreds he photographed of her.

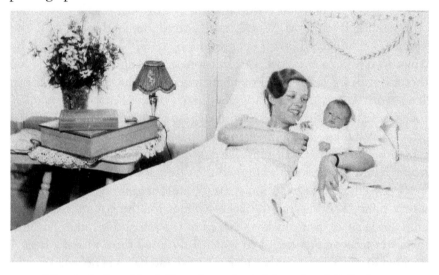

**Mary, in bed holding her daughter, just 2-3 days
after delivering Nancy into the world.**

Some months later, my grandparents and uncle with lights and cameras descended upon us in Waynesboro. There is the typical grandparents and baby pose: the four generations and numerous others. I even had my hair done for a glamor shot to send to Korea. And of course, a photo of mother's cocker spaniel, the regal Duke, sitting in his favorite chair. Those were pleasant days. When the baby fell off the bed for the first time, I was confident she had broken every bone, but my mother reassured me that the baby was too chubby from my milk and rice cereal to even have a bruise. It was a lesson for me, not for her, because once she learned how to roll over, she did it time and time again. Not on Nana's bed, however, unless she is under watch or surrounded by piles of pillows.

I wrote John often. His replies were infrequent and his letters often came two or three at a time. I knew from the newspapers sometimes where his division was, but of course, due to censorship, no details at all. I was shocked one day when a box identified as containing medals came in the mail. He had received the Purple Heart and a Bronze Star with two oak leaf clusters.

To this day, I don't know the details. Even the citation is not clear. All he ever said about the war was that his jeep driver was killed while driving him somewhere. When he came home in May, 16 months after leaving, I met him in Washington, D.C. and we had our postponed honeymoon. The baby was safely in the care of Gran, as my mother preferred to be called, and Aunt Gara.

Shortly afterward, as an engineer, he was assigned to Fort Leonard Wood again, the headquarters for the engineer corps. We lived in a small house in Lebanon, Missouri, about equidistant to the Fort as was Rolla, although in an opposite direction. Coming home, especially that particularly hot summer, was difficult for him. He had a long drive, long hours, and was training more raw recruits, doubtless testing his patience. Although we had been together only three months as a married couple, we were both different now in so many important ways. The baby took my attention away from him. She was old enough to know he was a stranger, and sometimes was uneasy around him. He was only 24 years old then but had lost half his hair while in Korea.

One day as I was cooking dinner, he said," I hope that isn't rice, I don't ever want a box of rice in the house." He was short tempered, then repentant. Then angry and not repentant. Nevertheless, we had another child less than a year later, and another one, both boys; then five and one half years later, our fourth child. We moved to Kansas City in 1963 after he had completed his obligatory four years of service and more. He resigned because we had two children in school, and the constant moving was hard on all six of us.

By the time of our divorce in 1968 we had moved 26 times in 16 years. My family, except my mother, had said to stay together because of the children. She never voiced her opinion, but I am certain she would have disagreed with that advice. She would have been right. She knew me better than I knew myself, at least at the time. And I think she knew the signs of an unhappy marriage, although I never wrote or told her about John's bizarre behavior.

My sister, Carol, just 16 months younger than me, also had four children and a failing marriage. I sometimes feel guilty about the pain that I, or both of us, must have caused our parents with the unwise marriages we made. Carol lived in Texas near our father, who had since remarried. His new wife's birthday, coincidentally was the same as our mother's. I wonder if he ever forgot his new wife's birthday! She had a five- year- old son, whom my father adopted. While he never said so, I think he would have liked to have a son of his own. Now he had the son he had always wanted.

Our mother, to her credit, never spoke a spiteful or mean word about the new Mrs. Greef. Perhaps she was not jealous, and may have even felt sorry for the new wife. My mother was well liked by the people of Waynesboro and respected as a businesswoman. I do think

Mary, about age 60

my mother was in love discreetly with a married man, but I doubt if they ever had an intimate relationship. Waynesboro was a small town, and my mother had her reputation to maintain. She did, however, take to having her nightly cocktail which may have been more than one. My sister, Gara, the younger one, intimated that several times. But mother never missed opening her office and doing her job, despite any unhappiness or depression she might be experiencing. Her letters, always typed, were full of news of people I had long forgotten about and cheery in tone.

I made one last visit with the children in 1962 when we were moving to Michigan from South Carolina. John had resigned from the army after his obligatory four plus years and joined Black and Veatch Engineers in Kansas City. He drove us to Waynesboro but did not stay because he had to return to Greenville, S.C. where the site of the water plant he was in charge of building. It was a nice visit, but slightly strained as the oldest child was six and the youngest one, just over one year. So the children did not know Gran, and Gran was not used to four little ones under her feet. I wonder if my mother and I even knew each other, at this stage in our lives.

Gara was away at college. Carol and I both knew our marriages were precarious, but in our usual family tradition, we didn't talk much, if at all, about it. I would have had to confess my mother was right in her assessment of the lack of compatibility between John and me. I doubt if I had told her about his change in personality. Today, I would diagnose that he probably suffered PTSD from his war experiences. Somehow, we had a nice visit, and the children were able to associate a face with the name, "Gran." My mother was afraid of flying, so it was out of the question for her to come visit us in Michigan or to Kansas City, our next assignment. As for making any long drive by herself, that was impossible.

I don't recall any one saying that having children would make you happy. As I reminisce about my own relationship with my mother, I wonder how many days I made her happy. Or how many unhappy days she experienced, due to my actions. I hope the feelings of both days at least balanced. I would like to hear her say, the happy days readily tipped the scales. In retrospect, I am sure I will be able to say the same about my brood.

As I look back at the memories which are now flooding my mind, I realize fully what a wonderful mother she was…an amazing person.

One night in 1971, she called me. How could I have fathomed that it was the night she would die? She said she was going home from the hospital the next day. She'd had some problem with her heart that had been taken care of. We talked a long time about a lot of things. I felt very close to her that night.

WE ARE OUR MOTHERS' DAUGHTERS

At six a.m. a call came from the hospital. She had died during the night. She was 67-years-old. That age, 67, seems young to me now that I am almost 20 years older than she was when she died.

Tears fill my eyes now as I think back on her call.

I genuinely regret that she died when she did. We lived far appart the last 20 years of her life. And, she missed the opportunity to see her daughters mature into the women she would have wanted us to become.

I had four young children, was divorced, and airplane travel could be afforded by the few. Our visits therefore came perhaps only every four to five years. We wrote often, and I always hurriedly slit open her envelopes. To my recent surprise, in searching through a forgotten box, I found a large packet of my letters I had written her from my college days. She had saved them, and at some time long ago, had given the packet to me. I often agree with those who besmirch email as being so temporary and flitting. Letters beg to be bound with ribbons and kept secreted away for years.

How can I ever thank her for who she was and what she did. In retrospect, and that is how we have to assess the past, our mother was a good parent. She put our well being and interests first. She wanted us to have the advantages of a good life. She was beautiful, intelligent and had a strong sense of values that we could use to guide our lives if we chose.

I think the qualities her German ancestors possessed in leaving the familiar and intimacy of family life, to make the dangerous voyage to a new country with a different language and customs were a big part of our mother's character. She had the courage and foresight to leave a life that was comfortable, but also unhappy. She sought a new vista in which she was successful despite the many challenges that new life presented.

She had inherited a good sense of values from her parents, disapproving of dishonesty or lying. Always insisting upon the truth. Being fair with others and true to yourself, at least, once you find out who you are.

But, who knows what a long retirement into old age might have been like for her. Her life might have become lonely, or her health may have slowly deteriorated. She may have sensed that while in the hospital, and lost her will to live. I will never know.

But this I do know.

It has been 45 years since her death…45 years for me to feel gratitude for all the sacrifices she made for us…45 years for me to appreciate the love, inspiration, and courage she demonstrated…45 years, yes, to place her in the place of honor she deserves. She was the one who "set the example."

Thank you, Mother.

Here is what **Nancy Cramer** has done to set the example.

She married and raised four children who were named after their ancestors: 1) Sara Margaret Stovall Hodges; 2) Jefferson Pence Stovall; 3) Nancy Caroline Stovall Anderson; and a beloved John Edward Stovall (1957-1975) who died in a tragic car-train accident [and for whom a scholarship for a golfer was established 35 years ago, he was an avid golfer and had been medalist that day].

She was divorced; took 48 hours of classes to obtain her elementary teaching certificate; taught school, both elementary, junior college and university while attending the local university to receive two advanced degrees in counseling.

Six years later she married a good man for a marriage that lasted 22 years until he took his life due to Alzheimer's.

Nancy retired then from her school counseling position and private practice for which she had obtained her Missouri counselor license, ans took over ownership and management of her husband's fire suppression company. She was only the second woman in Missouri to do this.

While teaching, she had been active in leadership positions in Missouri NEA at local and state level; then assumed similar positions with business and not-for-profit organizations. During a 20-year period she was fortunate to make 65 trips to about 50 countries, and shared those trips through travel logs with any group that invited her. She has received numerous awards from participation in MNEA, the Northeast Chamber, and in teaching. She was named Missouri Science Teacher the same week her son was killed.

She said, "I realized then what really matters in life. It's not the awards, but who you love and who loves you in return. I packed the awards away recently with feelings of nostalgia and especially, with sadness. Again in retrospect, it is revealing how much my life parallels my mother's life. Did I imitate her consciously? I don't think so, but the genes and the examples are here within me.

"I sold the business and retired at age 80. The next month I began five years and still continuing, as a volunteer at the National World War I Museum and Memorial. I wrote and published four books about WWI, and many articles for local newspapers and the internet about various topics. I am working on my fifth book about the heroic retreat of the Serbian Army in 1915. I met and began a relationship with the most compatible man I've ever known. I've been a member of Twyla Dell's delightful group of women companions since 1998. Their emotional support and intellectual stimulation have helped bring my life to completion.

"Seems like there is always something new that life has planned for me. I just have to open the right door ...AND SET AN EXAMPLE!"

WE ARE OUR MOTHERS' DAUGHTERS

6

Actions Speak Louder than Words

CAROLINE RUTH MYERS LINCOLN

September 30, 1897 — September 17, 2009

By Rowena Adaline Lincoln Hardinger

My mother, Caroline Ruth Myers, was born on a farm 10 miles north east of Oklahoma City to George (Ted) McClellan and Lizzie Ireton Myers. Her brother, Curt, was two years older. The selection of the beautiful farm site with house on a hill overlooking the 160-acre prairie was acquired by my grandfather when he was only 18 years of age.

On April 12, 1889, the gun fired at high Noon permitting a host of those seeking a new life in the relinquished territory to stake their land. They were called "Boomers". Ted was one of them who rode his pony searching for a site to own a part of the land.

109

WE ARE OUR MOTHERS' DAUGHTERS

At the gun firing, many hundreds of settlers came on horseback and in wagons to acquire the deed if they tended and lived on the land. Federal officers were interspersed through the crowd to spot the "Sooners" who had come earlier than the starting gun to possess the land. Eventually, many court cases were developed by Sooners to retain their land, but generally, the Sooner, realizing that he would be ordered to move, did so. That was the case of my grandfather, Ted Myers, born in 1871.

Ted first staked out land in Oklahoma City, but authorities told him this land had been set aside for school land and eventually for the state fair. Since it was public property he would have to move on. The sun was setting, and still no claim for Ted. He was even 10 miles northeast of the city when he spied a burning campfire and followed the smoke to find a farmer. Ted, who looked younger than his 18 years, rode up and the man said, "Kid, I did come in too soon. I'll have to get out. What will you give me for the land?" Ted Myers dug into his pocket and produced a 10-dollar gold piece, offering it. The Sooner accepted the exchange, and with a hand shake, Ted had a 160-acre farm overlooking the North Canadian River Bottom. This became his dwelling place for the remainder of his life.

Estimates of the "Boomers" ranged from 50,000 to 100,000. Congress had failed to provide for any form of civil government. A nearby town, Guthrie, unlike Rome that was not built in a day, was built in half a day! The night before April 12, 1889, the prairie roamed with coyote, gray folk and deer. By the evening the city was laid out, town lots staked off, the steps were taken to form a municipal government. Ten thousand people lit campfires for the night to resume building their houses the next day.

Ted settled on his new 160 acres, built a sod house of available clay. He went back to Arkansas City, Kansas, where he was raised. His parents had come from Pennsylvania. His mother, Martha Jane, was short and stocky, called Mrs. 5X5. Her husband, Peter Myers, was tall and lanky. They make quite a spectacle when together at family picnics and church meetings. Martha Jane was also a midwife and delivered children of relatives and local families.

Ted could not wait to tell Lizzie of his new adventure in Oklahoma. Lizzie was born in Kansas on June 3, 1871. Her father,

110

Phineas A. Ireton, was born July 17, 1838, in New Jersey. He was orphaned and raised by a Buchanan family, said to be related to President James Buchanan. He moved to Ohio, and on to Kansas. He became a teacher in the communities of Arkansas City and Chandler, Oklahoma, where he lived.

When Lizzie Ireton was born, she weighed only 2 ½ pounds, and her twin, Lillian, died. Even without modern technology equipment, family members were able to save Lizzie, using the warm stove oven and constant care to keep her alive.

Lizzie grew up on the Kansas farm. Two years before she was married, her father, Phineas Ireton, gave her a Bible with an inscription in beautifully shaded penmanship that read: "As a mark of parental affection, and in the hope that she may derive instruction and happiness from its study, this Bible is presented to Lizzie C. Ireton by her father, Phineas A. Ireton."

Lizzie had kept her promise to wait for him while he explored the Oklahoma land possibility. My grandmother told me that she remembered so well the first time he kissed her. They were married in Wichita, on April 26, 1893. He presented to her a solid gold ring, later inherited by her great grand-daughter, Ruth Hardinger. Lizzie was 22 years old as was Ted.

Ted and Liz moved to the new farm, and Ted continued to develop the land and living conditions. Soon he built the house on the hill that was home for his family. It was wood framed with a wide veranda porch in front and in back, a necessity for cooling off in Oklahoma's summer heat. The living room faced east, behind it, the dining room, and to the west, the kitchen with windows looking over the outhouse, vegetable garden and the windmill about 100 feet down the hill. The nearby hand pump provided water that was carried by bucket to the house. Three bedrooms were upstairs. The family began to increase when a son, Curtis Cecil Myers, was born Feb. 5, 1894, only five years after the Land Rush. Two years later, my mother, Caroline Ruth Myers was born, Sept. 30, 1897.

The Myers and Ireton parental families also moved to Oklahoma and settled near their children. The families were a part of the Pioneering Days of both Kansas and Oklahoma. Both grandfathers were involved in "freighting" – overland hauling cattle from Texas to northern states or markets in Kansas City and Dodge City, KS. They would be away from home weeks at a time, and the women endured the hardships and loneliness of the new settlement. Ruth's grandmother revealed to her that once an Indian knocked at her door and asked to see her man. She told him, "He has just stepped out." The Indian left.

The Indians were not a sovereign and independent nation, therefore, they were under the sole jurisdiction of not the state but the federal government. White settlers encroached on the Indian settlements in the Southeastern states. President Andrew Jackson in 1830 proposed removal of Indian tribes in Tennesee and Georgia to set up their own tribal government and move to Oklahoma to be placed on Reservations. Details of that march are tragically reported in the "Trail of Tears" stories of the trek.

Individual Indians were allowed to sell unoccupied lands they claimed to be their own to the Boomers who were anxious to enter Indian Territory, but the later Act of 1889 amendment to the Indian Appropriations Act, allowed President Benjamin Harrison to be involved in his historic bill that proclaimed unassigned lands be open to white settlers under much less stringent rules. Regarding the appropriation of city planning and Indian settlement, this comment was made in *The Harper's Weekly* observer reported less than a month later:

"It documents the massive stupidity of federal policy with regard to the disposal of the public domain, but it scarcely more than hints at the tragic consequences to follow for the Indian tribes who had been forcibly relocated to Oklahoma under solemn promises that their land   would be theirs forever."

Harper's Weekly 33 (May 18, 1889): 391-94

There were no schools at first, but when the children came along, settlers established schools. A little red brick school, Sunnyside, was a short distance down the red clay road from my mother Ruth's home on the hillside. There was only one teacher for the eight grades. Ruth started school when she was 5, "because the teacher was kind enough to put up with me." Her dad was on the school board, and he had the key to the schoolhouse. She became interested in the library, and read all the books twice or more that they shelved. She and Curt walked home for lunch and mother Lizzie would prepare bread pudding with sweet sauce, one of their favorites. One year a very good looking teacher was hired. She was courted by Dr. Earnhart from Spencer, OK. They married, and that was the end of her teaching career, for married women didn't teach.

Ruth's grandmother Ireton liked to read, as did her husband, Phineas, a teacher in both Kansas and Oklahoma. When Grandmother Martha Myers, who lived with the family, was too feeble to write, Ruth wrote the letters for her to Aunt Meg who lived on the turnpike in Circleville, OK.

When Ruth graduated from the country school, her parents sent her to 9th grade at Oklahoma City High. Because Ruth was homesick, her mother, Lizzie, went to live with her during the week for her first year. They found a light housekeeping apartment. Demonstrating his commitment to the arrangement, Ted drove the horse and buggy for a 2 -hour, a ten- mile trip each week. Ruth sang in the school chorus, took French and thrived with the many challenging classes.

Ted made his living farming. He kept his desire to raise corn and hogs from his northern background. Once he won an organ for the best bushel of corn at the State Fair. The organ was powered by foot pedals. A roller device with punctured dots turned to play a tune. Ruth took lessons on the organ until she got a new piano. Then, she took lessons from a teacher in Spencer, OK. At a lesson, she remembers being frightened for the teacher's baby had a spasm. The baby revived after her teacher put her into the bathtub.

Mother and her family visited her Aunt and Uncle who lived on a farm near Arkansas City, KS. They went to Oklahoma City and took the Santa Fe train. It was luxurious for them to ride the train, for the "news butch" would come through the aisles and sell all sorts of newspapers, toys, candy, vases, and slippers. Aunt Ida married a Scotch Presbyterian and she remembers his having family prayers each morning. Aunt Ida served tomato gravy and biscuits for breakfast that has become a Lincoln family favorite. They had three children and all had such fun together, continuing visits as adults.

One New Year's Eve, Ruth asked a friend to spend the night and they had permission to watch the clock with a cuckoo that would appear at the stroke of twelve. Both girls climbed up a step stool onto the table to watch the reliable bird announce the new year. Just as the cage door opened, the bird appeared with one chirp, Ruth punched her friend and said, "There he goes!" The girl immediately fell off the table, and took Ruth with her, missing the chimes announcing the New Year!

At age eight, Ruth remembers when Oklahoma became a state in 1905. Her family subscribed to *The Daily Oklahoman*, delivered to their mailbox a quarter of a mile away. Governor Haskell and his cohorts went to Guthrie and got the Oklahoma Seal and took it to Oklahoma City, declaring that this was the official capitol.

Oklahoma A&M was her choice of college in 1916. She declared a major in Home Economics, and lived in a girls' dorm with curfew. The ROTC was on campus, so she awoke to the playing of "Reveille" in the morning and went to bed to "Taps." She joined Kappa Delta Sorority, becoming a founding member of Nu Chapter and helped facilitate a new house on campus. She graduated in 1919, three years and two summers later with a Life Teaching Certificate and degree in Home Economics. She taught at a unionized rural school in Luther, about 12 miles east of Oklahoma City. They had four teachers in high school, all with degrees, which was rare at that time. The school was rated as the best rural school in the United States that year.

Ruth was 23 years old when the 19th Amendment was ratified, August 18, 1920. Ted was happy that both the women in his family could vote for President Woodrow Wilson.

After the first year, the dean of home economics at Oklahoma State University asked Mother to join the faculty in Teacher Training, helping new teachers meet the challenges of their job. Dean Talbot asked Mother to a party, and she met Ben A. Lincoln. They both came with other partners, but a friendship developed between them. He had graduated from the University of Arkansas in Fayetteville after World War I, and worked at OSU supervising on-the-job agricultural training. They were married about a year later at the Presbyterian Church in Stillwater, Oklahoma on July 12, 1924. Dean Talbot presented the couple with wooden candlesticks, now my treasure. They decorated the church in wild flowers including sun flowers collected from the roadside. The wedding was held at eight o'clock in the morning, for it was hot by mid-day in July. The President of OU, Bradford Knapp's wife had a bridal party. Ruth remarked, "I think people who get married in July are a little lacking in their intelligence." Mrs. Knapp retorted, "Well, that's when we got married!" The young couple honeymooned at Lake Taneycoma in Missouri.

The newlyweds moved to Little Rock where Ben worked for the Veterans Administration, giving agricultural assistance to returning veterans interested in farming in Arkansas. I am their oldest daughter, Rowena Adaline Lincoln, born in St. Vincent's Hospital, where later my brother, Benjy, operated as a surgeon. After two years in Little Rock, Ben took a job as County Agricultural Agent in Paragould, AR. This is where Benjamin Myers Lincoln and Lucy Carolyn Lincoln were born.

With home economics background, Mother knew organized play for young children was an important part of their world. She arranged a kindergarten group that met in our home. The living room with its coalburning stove for heat, was turned into a play area for the 6–10 youngsters, including the Lincoln children, for activities. Kindergarten for public schools came much later.

During the Depression, 1933, the family moved back to Little Rock. Ben supervised a program that dispensed fresh meat to poverty victims.

As the economy improved, Ben and Ruth moved to Batesville, Arkansas, into a green frame house at 510 Harrison Street, just across from the elementary school. Ben was the new County Agricultural Agent with his assistant, Reece Dampf, who had also boarded with and assisted the former agent. Reece needed a place to live, and he asked Ruth if he could continue to live in the same house with them. Mother replied that they had three children and three bedrooms, and there wasn't room. Reece replied, "Well, I could sleep upstairs with Bud." (my brother Benjy age 7 or 8 at the time) Reece became a member of the family who stayed with us, ate with us, brought his dates to our home, and eventually his wife and lifetime companion. Reece was drafted in World War II, and served in the European theater. After the war, he and Eloise traveled for US Aid to

International Development (USAID) in many countries as ambassadors and agricultural educators. Eloise wrote copious single spaced type written letter of their many adventures, stimulating an interest in travel in all of us. She was also the matron of honor in our wedding.

Eventually, the Lincolns moved to a more spacious home, 1141 South Main in Batesville. We had a large back yard. Ben milked a Jersey cow, providing rich nourishment for four growing children. Ruth made cottage cheese and sold it at the nearby grocers.

The Lincoln family (L-R):
Lydia, Ben, Ruth, Lucy, Benjy, Rowena

Customers would ask for, "Mrs. Lincoln's cottage cheese." We also had a big vegetable garden, and we learned to enjoy eating many vegetables as well as skills to grow and prepare them. Mother Ruth employed Negro girls who came from the countryside to go to the Negro High School. She encouraged their education. One special helper was named Gertie May Norga Lee Watkins. She told us her family had 13 children, and all had four names! Ruth did quite a bit of canning, and eventually freezing. Yet, Ben was in the 'dog house' when he brought home a bushel of over- ripe peaches on a Saturday night. Ruth moaned, thinking of getting peaches canned that night and their kids off to Sunday school the next morning. It all happened with teamwork.

Often it was expedient for Ben to bring associates home with him for lunch with the Lincolns, and Ben loved to show off his family. Mother greeted each new guest and we would sit down for the usual family meal. If we were short of any food, mother would give the signal, "FHB" which meant, Family Hold Back, for we didn't have enough to go around. "MIK" meant More in the Kitchen. One guest passed the bread, an FHB item, and insisted I take a piece. I politely said, "No thank you." After he insisted, I looked at Lucy and she giggled, then Benjy did, as did Lydia. Although Ben hoped to present us as model children, this time we failed the test, for the guest had no clue as to our silly laughter! Mother Ruth took great pride in choice of food as well as preparation and serving for her family.

One evening, Ruth asked all of our teachers to the house for games and refreshments. In that way, we became acquainted with the teachers and they became real people to us children as they presided over the classroom. I remember asking Mother Ruth, "What can I do?" She gave to me a list so long I have never had to ask again!

With permission, I invited one special friend to come home from school with me for lunch to celebrate my 13th birthday. We were served lunch and my favorite, Grandma Pineapple Cake. Mary Jean and I walked back to afternoon classes.

Meanwhile my 42-year-old mother was expecting her fourth child and her physician, Dr. Johnson, had asked Ben to go bird-hunting with him, so both her confidants were out of town. She was experienced enough to know it was time for the new baby to arrive. Realizing it was the TIME, Ruth called Dr. Lamb who immediately transported her to Johnson Hospital. My father came home late afternoon, and announced that I had a new baby sister, Lydia Elizabeth Lincoln. What a birthday surprise for me! Even now, she is called the 'baby' of the family.

117

WE ARE OUR MOTHERS' DAUGHTERS

We four children all attended Batesville Public Schools. In 1940, an election was held to support building a new high school. Although many parents and citizens worked hard to pass the project, the vote failed. After I went to school the next day, a senior group decided that students should protest the decision. We skipped class, gathered in the school courtyard and marched downtown to support the proposal again, demanding that we needed a new high school. The school authorities persuaded us to return to class with threats of being expelled. I sheepishly walked home from school to relate the news of our march to town. I was sure of parental disapproval, but my mother, Ruth, said, "That is great! I am glad you participated! The parents tried, and now they heard from you students." I had a lesson in how democracy works – by expressing one's view and acting upon it. Eventually, the new school was built.

In 1941 Ruth and Ben thought it was time to expose the family to some of the wonders of the US. We set out on a three-week trip including Colorado, Yellowstone, California, through Death Valley and on to Carlsbad Cavern. Our car had no air conditioning, but we rolled down the windows and enjoyed seeing the scenery of the changing landscape patterns of our great country. We stayed in a cabin in Yellowstone, and Mother Ruth emptied the garbage in the can but encountered a black bear between her and cabin. She shooed him away!

We stopped for gas along the way, and each of the family got out to stretch and explore the country store with its many isles of merchandise. We piled back into the car and Mother began driving for Dad, not feeling well. stretched out in the back seat among the children. About 2 miles down the road, someone exclaimed, "Where's Lydia?" Without even an answer to the question, Dad sat up from the back seat, mother made a U turn in the middle of the highway, they exchanging drivers. Dad sped back to the station. Two- year old Lydia was sitting on the counter with a pink sucker in her mouth. The attendant told her that her parents would soon return. Whew! We all felt guilty for that overlook! It took several years for this to become a favorite funny family story.

After my graduation from Batesville High School in 1943 my Aunt Adaline Lush came to Batesville from Ames, Iowa, and

118

invited me to attend Iowa State University and live with their family. Uncle Jay Lush was a genetics professor. It was difficult to leave my home and family in Arkansas, but following Mother Ruth's footsteps, I accepted the challenge and graduated in home economics in 1947.

In the summer of 1944, my father, Ben, was offered a position similar to the one he had after World War I, and the family moved back to Little Rock, Arkansas. He worked with Veterans Administration, helping World War II veterans find positions in agriculture. Farming was competitive and ten cents a bird was good profit in the chicken industry, demanding a large production from farmers. Ben worked with some of his former colleagues who had previously stayed in Little Rock.

All three of the other Lincoln children graduated from Little Rock Central High. Benjy chose medicine. He graduated from University of Arkansas in Fayetteville, and then went to Little Rock Medical College in Little Rock, serving his intern residency in open-heart surgery at Kansas City General. He preferred more general surgery and established a private practice in Little Rock for many years.

After graduation from Little Rock Central High, Lucy chose the University of Arkansas where her father, Aunt Adaline, Bert Lincoln, and her brother, Benjy, had graduated. Lydia also attended the University of

Ruth, Mother of the Year, 1961

119

Arkansas, graduated in 1958. All three of the Lincoln sisters majored in home economics.

Mother Ruth continued her work at Second Presbyterian Church, where she became a 50+ year member, also a member of League of Women Voters, and American Association of University Women. She renewed many friendships and loved to play bridge. The couple enjoyed overseas travel to many countries with friends. They also delighted in the role of grandparenting 12 grandchildren, assisting with new arrivals.

Ben and Ruth decided in the late 60's to move to Ben's family farm in Van Buren, Arkansas. However, Mother did not want to live on the farm, so they lived in the first house they ever built on Lincoln Hill, about 5 miles from the farm. Daddy Ben loved to tend his herd of Angus cattle and named the calves after the grandchildren. When the children visited, they delighted in dropping bales of hay from the pickup truck onto the pasture, with cattle following the hay.

Ruth and Ben's retirement also brought on the care for two elderly relatives. Lizzie Myers came to live with them most of her life after Ted died. Also, Lydia Turman, Ben's half-sister who raised him when his mother died, lived in Van Buren. After Lydia's fall, Ben give her the choice of going to a nursing home or living with them, and she chose the latter. Both of the aged family members died in the Lincoln home in Van Buren. Both Ruth and Ben vowed they would never live with their children. They came for frequent visits, but chose not to live with any of us.

Ruth continued her interest at First Presbyterian Church in Ft. Smith as well as other national organizations. In 1961, she represented Arkansas as Mother of the Year at the Waldorf Astoria in New York City. She and Ben enjoyed meeting other state's Mothers and the elegance of the city. They took several overseas tours with friends and related the experiences to the family.

Ben A. Lincoln died October 1, 1973, in his home in Van Buren under the care of their doctors in Little Rock. He was buried in the family plot in Van Buren's Gill Cemetery.

Ruth, 108-Years-Old

When Ruth was 90 years old, she decided to move back to Little Rock to be nearer her family. An apartment was found at Parkway Village. Each birthday after 90, the family aassembled and celebrated her adding another year. For one birthday, her retirement complex provided a horse and carriage, and she was driven around the complex grounds. Residents clapped, and all celebrated with an ice cream treat. Another year, the family took a boat ride up the Arkansas River, viewing the city and bridges from the water. At her 110th birthday, she was helped to the seat of the helicopter and the pilot flew her over the city. The greats and grand children were much entertained with the mechanics of the helicopter as they inspected the interior of the craft before she took off with the rotating propellers lifting her to the clouds above us.

Returning from a trip my husband and I had made to Thailand, I presented Mother Ruth a silver elephant necklace. She said, "Rowena, I can't wear this, I am a Democrat!" She was 109 years old at that time.

Mother enjoyed explaining her Oklahoma history to students at the Clinton Presidential Center in Little Rock and answered questions about her interesting pioneer background. At 110 years of age, she was also the oldest graduate of Oklahoma State and had an oral history interviewed, recorded for an OU Library project by Tanya Finchum and Juliana Nykolaiszyn.

Caroline Ruth Myers Lincoln died Sept. 17, 2009, in Little Rock, approximately the thirtieth oldest person in the world. She was 111 + 352 days old. She was buried in the family plot in Gill Cemetery in Van Buren, sharing the same tombstone with Ben A. Lincoln, giving their birth, death, and marriage dates. Condolences were sent by many friends of many races and ages to help the family through their grieving process of our beloved Mother Ruth.

Although Mother Ruth gave much sage advice through the years, her life demonstrated many of her dynamic traits she considered important and passed them on to family and others. She regarded her faith as paramount in keeping an orderly and focused life to promote wellbeing. She sought good health in food choices, exercise, and games. She had a professional life, teaching at Oklahoma University. It was her choice to become Ben's wife and raise children. She fostered education, and learning skills helpful to meet these standards, as exemplified in each of her children seeking professional skills. Each of their daughters majored in home economics and has made many contributions to the communities where they lived. Their son had an illustrious career as a surgeon in Little Rock. Over all, she approached these goals with good humor stating, "Most things that are fun in life are either illegal, immoral, or fattening."

Born on January 31, 1926, Rowena was the first child of Caroline Ruth Myers and Benjamin A. Lincoln. One son and two daughters completed their family. The family lived in Little Rock, Paragould and Batesville, Arkansas, where she graduated from high school in 1943. Her Aunt Adaline Lincoln Lush, asked her to come to Ames and live with their family. Iowa State has a high rating in her chosen field of home economics. Her first summer job away from home was at College Camp on beautiful Lake Geneva, WI, in the Craft Department.

At ISU, she joined Kappa Delta, the same national sorority as her mother at Oklahoma University. At the Snowball Dance, she met a handsome returning GI, Loren Hardinger. and they dated for over a year. They were married after graduation in 1947 in Little Rock, and moved to his family home in Albia, Iowa. That fall, she taught home economics in the high school, where Loren had graduated in 1942.

She resigned after teaching two years. In 1950, their daughter, Ruth Ann Hardinger, was born. They purchased an acreage a mile from the city square. Jon Lincoln Hardinger was born in 1953, and David Loren in 1954. In 1962, the family built their dream home using Frank Lloyd Wright ideas from a house-planning course at ISU.

A teaching offer was made at the new Lincoln Junior High in Albia and that became a challenge. In 1971, Title IX brought boys into the formerly girls home economics classes. Rowena pursued a MS program at ISU, developing lesson plans in nutrition.

After 27 years of teaching, she and her husband traveled the 50 states and over 50 foreign countries. They also made frequent trips to New York City where daughter, Ruth Hardinger and husband Michael Norton have developed art careers.

The couple selected Tucson, Arizona, for winters, enjoying the activities of their energetic senior community. She learned skills in watercolor painting and participated in the American Association of University Women. Loren died there in 2011. Rowena moved from their winter residence in Albia to Cedar Falls, IA, to be nearer two sons and their families.

7

If I let it get to me,
I knew I would have gone crazy myself

ANNE (GOLDBERG) GILBERT

June 26, 1908	—	October 17, 2003
Boston, Massachusetts		Boston, Massachusetts

By Marian Leah Knapp

Am I My Mother's Daughter?

What a monumentally historic day it was for women when Hillary Clinton accepted the nomination for President at the 2016 Democratic National Convention.

WE ARE OUR MOTHERS' DAUGHTERS

She said:

"Standing here as my mother's daughter, and my daughter's mother, I'm so happy this day has come. When any barrier falls in America, for anyone, it clears the way for everyone."

I can only reflect on my own experience as my mother's daughter and not on "my daughter's mother." I am the mother of sons, but if Hillary had male offspring it would have been an historic day for them as well. Hillary is right in saying that any breached barrier will benefit all, except perhaps for those who wish to retain, shore-up, or build fences to keep others from achieving their dreams.

So, with these ideas in mind, I think about my mother, Anne (Goldberg) Gilbert. She didn't have a middle name because her mother was too worn out to think of one. My mom was born in Boston, Massachusetts on June 26, 1908 and she died on October 17, 2003 in Boston, at age 95. In between her birth and death, she lived most of her adult life with my father, Lou, in Providence, Rhode Island, where I was born and raised. Anne was the daughter of Jewish immigrants who came to America in the late 1800s to escape poverty, oppression, and the omnipresent specter of death at the hands of the Tsarist Russian Empire, simply because they were Jews. Her parents, grandparents, and many other relatives came, as millions of others did, in dribs and drabs. Newly arrived immigrants repeatedly sent money to those still in the old country to buy steerage tickets for the voyage across the ocean. Once here, no one ever thought about going back. That miserable life was over. As hard as it was in the New World, it was better than the terrifyingly tentative existence in Russia.

My grandmother, Minnie, bore eleven children in America. Eight of them lived into adulthood. Anne was the third youngest child and by the time she was old enough to remember, her mother had stopped taking care of her. Maybe it was because of the death of children and the daily struggle to put food on the table, but Minnie seemed to have broken apart. Her behavior was erratic and scary. She yelled at people without cause, fought with her husband forcing him

126

to live in the basement of their rented triple-decker, and she threw bottles at passing cars because they were too noisy. From a very young age, every Friday afternoon, Anne, with her younger sister took a ferry from East Boston to the West End where their tiny, very old, blind grandmother bathed them, washed and combed their hair, cooked dinner, and baked thumb-print cookies. She knew that her daughter, Minnie, wasn't properly watching out for them.

When I was old enough to want to understand my mom's history, I asked her how she managed to live through the menacing atmosphere at home. "I just ignored it," she said. "If I let it get to me, I knew I would have gone crazy myself."

In my mind, this one sentence frames the persona that my mother carried with her throughout her life. Her personality was both realistic and practical. She saw with great clarity what was going on around her, but she had the capacity to hover over the difficulties and look for optimistic solutions. This characteristic was valued by everyone who knew her. When there was a problem people came to her and she responded. When a sister tried to commit suicide several times she always went to take care of her. When a sister-in-law died, she was a second mom to her young niece. When a nephew had to be admitted to a state mental health institution, my mom, along with my dad, were there to shore up her sister and brother-in-law.

It wasn't so much what my mother said to me about what was a good way to live. It was more what I saw her do. She embodied a set of values that I don't think she would have been able to define herself. She just did what she did and I watched, listened, and absorbed her reactions into me.

I was a very adorable, small little girl – sweet and gentle. In my neighborhood the man who had a store on a nearby corner liked me. He was large, bulky, and overpowering. When he would see me he would draw me into a suffocating bear-like hold. It scared me and I told my mother. She didn't ignore my worries; she didn't say "he doesn't mean anything by it," or "let's not make a fuss." She took me by the hand and we walked together to the shop, so I could witness her actions. "Marian doesn't like it when you hug her," she said. I remembering him sputtering as he said, "I don't mean anything by it!

127

She is just so cute." "That's fine," my mom said, "but don't touch her anymore." That was the end of it. He never hugged me again.

When I was 10 years old, I won the first place award in a prestigious children's art contest. The school system sponsored this competition where each elementary school could send one fifth-grade student to Saturday art classes at the Rhode Island School of Design. What an honor! RISD was one of Providence's major claims to fame. However, that was the year that our family was moving from one neighborhood to another into a larger flat, which meant that I would be going to a different school. Our cramped two-bedroom place had become too small for my parents and their three growing children. Because of the move to a new school, the authorities said that I could not get the award. I, and everyone else in my family, was crushed, and we fervently declared the unfairness of it all. Multiple times, my mom went to the decision-makers to argue on my behalf. She lost every time. There was some talk about my parents sending me anyway, but there was no money to pay for anything except our basic needs. Of course I was disappointed that I couldn't go to art school. But it wasn't until I was well into my adulthood that I realized that my mom gifted me with something much more important – how to stand up for what you believed. In this case that belief was in me.

Much later in my life, in the early 1970s, around the time the *Roe v. Wade* question on abortion was being debated in the U.S. Supreme Court I talked with my mother, who at the time was in her early 60s, about the issue. My mom, with a fervor that I had rarely seen before, said, "No one has a right to tell a woman what to do with her own body!" She had seen her own mother have more children than she could take care of. She had been there when a sister had illegal abortions because she wasn't capable financially and emotionally to raise another child. Maybe she even knew that her mother-in-law had given herself at least one abortion with a hat pin. And she understood the daunting obstacles that women faced trying to have control over their own reproduction with the extremely limited options to prevent pregnancy. As a very young woman, I didn't really think too much about children, birth control, and abortion, but I knew the family history. I vaguely leaned towards the notion of choice. My mom's clear, unequivocal statement sealed my stance.

My mother always wanted to go to college to become a social worker. She was even accepted at Simmons College. But shortly before she graduated from high school (with honors) her father died and she had to find work to buy coal to heat the house.

I went well beyond her in education. Certainly I have learned a great deal, but I feel intensely that my academic learning is far inferior to the basic, common-sense, intuitive knowledge that is within me. I definitely got this quality from her. How lucky I am to have inherited that attribute from my mother. She didn't consciously pass this on, of course. She had no control over what would come out in the gene-pool mix. But I think I have it and it is what sustains me in all of the variations of my own life. It is my steadfast foundation.

Yes, I am my mother's daughter, but that does not mean that I am a clone of her. She was unique, just as I am the only me. I never had to live through the uncertainty of her childhood, her mother's rejection, and the struggle that she and her family went through to have shelter and food. I do share with her, mainly through osmosis, the impact of the Great Depression that taught me how every penny was a precious item to spend wisely. I saw her being involved with family, friends, and community in a helpful way, and I am sort of like that. She certainly advocated for people she loved and for causes that she

129

believed in, but she had to be selective on where she put her energy. I guess I do these things too.

So, in many ways then I am my mother's daughter. But I am also my father's daughter, my aunts' and uncles' niece. I am my siblings' sibling. I'm my sons' mother and mother-in-law to their wives. I am my grandchildren's grandma, and I am my friends' friend. All of these relationships have shaped me and continue to influence how I see and do things. I have incorporated pieces of all of them into me. But I have my own personality and my own way of reacting to, and integrating my encounters, and relationships into my being. Each of us is unique in that way. Any one of us may see the same event and each will react to it differently. We will find and take away lessons and meaningful messages depending on our personal perspectives and mindsets.

Over the years, I have spent bits of time here and there trying to recognize the ways in which I am the same or different from my mother. However, I can never conjure up a complete, comprehensive picture. Simply, that's because I never knew the totality of who she was. I cannot with complete assurance say that I really knew and understood her. I could hear what she said and watch what she did, but I didn't know all of her intimate thoughts, and the construct she had created for her inner self. So, I can say in a qualified way that I am my mother's daughter, but only related to my observations about who I think she was.

The passage of time informs the issue of whether I am my mother's daughter. As she aged and I aged along with her, we both changed. I grew in understanding and knowledge as she declined physically and mentally to a stage where she was just waiting to die. She did provide a model for aging and dying that I hope to replicate. She put all her affairs in order, made good decisions about not driving anymore, and moving to be closer to me so I didn't have to drive back and forth to Rhode Island to take care of her. Once she made those major changes, she was content to enjoy some social family times, and then gradually just let the clock tick out. That's what I want to do. So, maybe mom, I am your daughter.

Marian Leah (Gilbert) Knapp is a writer, community activist, and family devotee from Newton, Massachusetts. She has a bachelor's degree in English literature from Boston University, a master's degree from Hunter College in anthropology, and a Ph.D. from Antioch University New England in environmental studies. She serves as chair of her local Council on Aging, writes a regular column on aging for the Newton TAB, has published one book "Aging in Places: Reflective Preparation for the Future," and has a book on caregiving in production. You can read her writings on her website and blog, voicesofaging.com.

WE ARE OUR MOTHERS' DAUGHTERS

8

Treat People Fairly
And Love Children

Mildred Frances Mertz May

1908 Coplay, Pennsylvania—1999 Noxen, Pennsylvania

By Susan May Kuchinsky

I remember my mother as incredibly strong, patient, and classy. She had a wonderful sense of humor and at the same time had an air of mystery about her. She was a very attractive woman and had wonderful taste in clothes. When I view the family history of pictures, there is Mildred always looking beautiful no matter the situation. Short in stature with slim hips, legs, and arms, Mildred held a lot of her sex appeal in her face and in her large breasts. Of course this was before the age of implants.

Mother was a kind and generous person. One time when we were at the 5 and 10

133

cent store a little boy was two cents short for a Mother's Day gift. She reached over and handed the clerk the two cents. She got a big smile and a thank you from the little boy. She turned to me and said, "Be kind and treat people fairly." This was an important lesson for a nine-year-old.

Mildred completed grade nine and left school to work. She was the oldest of seven children, including twin boys who died in infancy. My mother had to leave school to support herself as my grandmother left the family and it fell apart. There was much shaming by my father for her not graduating from high school and he would bring this up during his rage episodes.

My mother spoke the Pennsylvania Dutch language fluently. She used to speak this with my great Aunt Elsie who lived close by. I can remember her singing songs to us in this language. "Hal da mal" meant "shut your mouth closed" is what I remember most as I was a talkative child. When she was approximately eighteen years old Mildred went to the Poconos, a resort area, to work for the summer. Here she met "colored" people as she called them for the first time. Mildred describes the work as very hard, but the people were great. She referred to one black woman as taking her under her wing and showing her the ropes. She spoke fondly of her experience with colored people. When the civil rights movement began and the dogs and water hoses were let loose on marchers, we knew where my mother stood.

That air of mystery came from her willingness to take risks despite being confined by poverty, abuse and sexism. In her 20s she managed to go Tunkhannock Airport, about 13 miles away and up for a ride with her uncle in a biplane in the mid-1930s. Her Uncle Miles took her up for the ride of her life though she didn't know it then. Later he gave her a Tennessee walking horse as a gift, which her husband sold for a tractor instead of putting in the bathroom he promised her in exchange for that beautiful horse. A bathroom would have been a fabulous gift to his wife, but he chose the tractor instead, something she would never sit on.

My father was a bigot and wanted all the freedom marchers in Alabama killed while my mother's values of kindness and fairness made much more sense to me. Mildred also shared that when she was married in 1928 the judge asked if she had any Negro blood in her. She replied, "not to my knowledge." If she had answered yes, the judge may have refused to marry them. Mother had a keen sense of justice and had insight into the social movements of our time.

Mildred bore children for 23 years. She was 20 when she had her first born and 43 when she had her last child. All children were born at home with the exception of the last one. Dad said, "A woman having a baby is like a cow having a calf." We were born at home with relatives as nurses. Marjorie, the last one, was born in the hospital in Meshoppen, Pennsylvania. Mother was pregnant before she was married in 1928. My father blamed that on her, too. A local doctor told mother that "all Tom has to do is hang his pants on the bedpost and she gets pregnant."

Tom had suffered abuse from his father who used to beat him with a horsewhip when he could not recite names and race times of harness-horse racing in the area. The abuse passed on as generational trauma. His own father lived in a shack and refused to work. My father broke the cycle by working from 1941 until retirement, mending that part of the pattern though the rest of the rage and alcoholism and abuse he poured out on his family.

Mildred breast fed all of her children for nine months, and they kept coming--with the first four boys and my oldest sister being lumped together age wise (1929 through 1937). There was a six-year gap between Barbara and Carolyn with Carolyn coming in 1943, me in 1946, and Marjorie in 1951. This six-year gap was explained when I was exposed to a big family secret at fifteen years of age. I was in the house alone with my parents when they began fighting. I stepped sidewise between them. My father walked over to the dining room and my mother to the kitchen. She said to him, "and you tried to ruin me too, having 15 children." He told her she was crazy and walked out of the house. Later that night I asked my mother about this. She told me she "got rid of seven children" during this time period. I asked her how she did this. She said that Aunt Elsie helped her. She took slippery elm and another herb which I cannot recall. This was hard for her as she loved children, but felt she had no other choice. She told me that she never wanted to talk about this again and that I was never to tell anyone about it, thus continuing the secret. I did not share this with my sisters until I was in my 50's and my brothers do not know about

135

this either. This was a profound experience for me considering the word "abortion" was not common place in 1961 and the act itself was also illegal.

Mildred in house dress and apron.

In a way the Great Depression defined my parents as it did that generation. My father was a journeyman electrician in 1928 and was working in Allentown, Pennsylvania. Here he met and married my mother Mildred Mertz.

The marriage had just gotten started when along came a baby and the Depression.

He took his family north to his family home in Noxen. My great Aunt Gertrude owned the small farm and over a period of years my parents purchased it from her. The house was built in 1872 and my grandfather was born there in 1875.

My father was out of work from 1929 through 1941. The two of them and the kids farmed the land and raised dairy cattle, horses, and chickens. They survived by working the farm, and also received government relief supports payments. Life was filled with hardships and the fatalism of poverty set in. Beliefs such as "try your best but chances are you will not get ahead," and "do not trust anyone" were endemic in the family system. The rigid social class system of the area and the success of extended family members also fed into these beliefs. When aunts, uncles, and cousins visited us, they always enjoyed my mom's cooking, but felt they were "slumming it" when they had to use the outhouse.

They would hold their noses and crack jokes about it. It embarrassed my mother terribly. They had wealth, she had regular beatings from her husband. We were looked down upon and I experienced this shaming one time when in second grade the zipper of a winter coat I had gotten from my first cousin, Jack, broke and I had to use safety pins. While standing in line to go out to recess, I fumbled with the safety pins. The teacher said to hurry up and that maybe next year my parents would see that I had a decent coat. Not only that, everyone knew that I had a boy's coat on as the gender differences in clothing were very apparent at that time. I remember crying and telling my mother about this. She just said that she was sorry and that I had to do the best that I could.

She wore dresses and aprons to do her housework since my father would not allow her to wear pants, shorts or sleeveless dresses. She was able to wear slacks later on her own, but the family existed on hand-me-downs and what we could buy on small accounts at stores in the nearest town. Like so many women of that generation, she sewed. Bags of feed turned into skirts and blouses and aprons.

When my father went to work in Allentown in 1941, we had a break from his abuse. The tension dropped and we could laugh and relax. Away from physical battering, the rages, and alcoholic binges, my mother let her humor and love of music take over. She also loved to dance. Mom would kick up her heels and do the Charleston or lead us around the living room in a waltz filling the room with music from radio and record player. She loved Elvis, and enjoyed a wide variety of music. She passed this love to me and supported my playing a cornet and baritone horn. I was a band student from 4th grade through high school. Band was my salvation as it got me out of the house during parades in the summer and football season, and provided a level of socialization for me. My father would not allow us to have friends over and especially boys could not visit our home. This isolation led to lack of friends and the lack of opportunity to have normal dating experiences. The boys were able to get out, but the girls were in essence "held hostage."

I remember when I was in the 9th grade, a senior band student asked me to the senior prom. My mom took a chance and had my Aunt Dot make me a beautiful green floral print chiffon dress with a cumberbund waist. It was just beautiful! I wore high heels and everything!! My dad was across the property when the boy and his parents came to get me. They wanted to take pictures. I tried to hurry them along. We left for the dance without confrontation. I had a good time at the dance. When I got home, Carolyn came out and got me, telling the boy not to get out of the car. When I walked into the house, I saw why. The door to the living room was busted up in pieces, and everyone was crying. He was a rage-aholic and let out his anger on the door.

Another rage episode from my father had occurred. The next day he told me that I was never to have anyone on the place again or he would kill them. He also told my mother that he would never touch her again. This incident sparked her to end their sexual relationship, as she said that she had apologized to him and accepted the blame as always. She told me she would never do that again and moved downstairs to sleep on the sofa sleeper. I think that hurting one of her daughters in this way was just too much for her. She was only 52 years old at the time. The next time I had a man on the place was when I introduced my father to my husband in 1966.

While my father was resting in his rented room or at my youngest brother's home in Allentown during the week, my mother had the responsibility of helping my brothers run the farm and raise the children. Mother wanted all of us to graduate from high school and we all did. Carolyn did drop out after her junior year, but later in life earned her GED certificate. How mother ever had time to read and sing to us, I will never know as she did so much physical labor.

We finally installed running water in the home in 1951, a gas stove in 1957, and a furnace in 1968, long after I left in 1964. My youngest brother put a bathroom in the house in 1982 after he observed my elderly father stumbling down the cellar steps. A shower and a toilet were installed in the cellar when I was nine years old. Every installation or improvement created a rage episode for which the whole family paid an emotional price.

My father worked hard too. When he came home on the weekends, he attacked his wonderful vegetable garden every summer. We all worked hard for winter food supplements. We canned 800 quarts of tomatoes, 800 quarts of string beans, and the same with peaches, pears, corn, applesauce, mustard pickle, and pickles were standard fare for the summer workload. We stored all this in the basement on groaning shelves and over the winter emptied the jars and made ready for the next season. My father would not invest in a freezer because of the cost of electricity.

Carolyn and I spent time watering plants, pulling weeds, and hoeing the garden. In 1946, we finally installed electricity and we grew up hearing from both of our parents to "turn off the lights" when leaving a room. My love of gardening comes from both of my parents. To this day I enjoy working in the yard.

Poverty loomed its ugly head in my family all of my mother's life. A major belief was that there was never enough. I think that during the Depression years starvation and losing the farm were a reality for my parents. Wearing hand-me- downs from other family members was expected and no one was ever to complain about it. My mother shoved her larger feet into used shoes sent to her by her sister. She developed corns from this and I remember her soaking her feet in Epson Salts to relieve the pain.

When I was about 14, my mother received some AT&T stock from her Aunt Eva. Aunt Eva worked as a ladies-room attendant for the Leheigh Valley Railroad and was able to earn railroad stock which she converted to AT&T stock. Upon her death mother received about $4,000.00 in stock. This was a huge windfall for her and allowed her to have some financial independence from my father. My father had given her $40.00 a week, and she was supposed to buy all of the groceries, pay the bills, and buy clothes for all of the children. Having some money of her own was an uplifting experience for my mother. She consulted an attorney about leaving him since she had acquired some money. The attorney said, "Mildred, you have three daughters to raise, 9,14, and 17. Pennsylvania would not look favorably about splitting the money. He could get it. I advise you to keep as quiet as possible about the money." She took his advice and stayed. My father did end up paying for the girls' dental bills. Both of my parents lost their teeth due to having no funds for dental care. Mother never went to a dentist for preventive care and lost her teeth throughout her life and got false teeth in midlife. They both got prescription glasses somehow.

During the 1960s my two oldest sisters worked in factories. They also paid mom some rent. When my oldest sister was 24, she bought a car. Mom had to sign for it as single women were not considered to be responsible enough to pay their debts. Having a car was another way to gain some independence.

No longer would my mother have to go into a bar in town and tell my father that the grocery and other shopping was done and that she was ready to go home. No longer would we have to sit in the back seat and be frightened that he was going to run off the road on the way home. When we had moments of freedom, it was such a powerful experience. These moments broke through those veils of poverty and abuse and demonstrated the presence of hope.

I graduated in 1964 and went to Missouri to pursue a college education. Having failed to get accepted at Pennsylvania colleges, a helpful guidance counselor suggested trying the Midwest, and I was accepted at Central Missouri State College in Warrensburg. For me to get there was another challenge. Again my mother helped me realize my dream. She asked my brother Miles to finance my education and he said yes! He paid for two years. I married in 1966 and completed my Bachelor of Science in Education in 1970. My mother's wonderful parenting skills (she was using time out long before the professionals labeled it), and her unconditional love of children were contributing factors to my success as a teacher and school counselor.

I will always remember how much she loved Christmastime. We would wake up to the house all cleaned and polished up, a turkey in the oven, and presents to be opened. She did it for her children, always the children. She suffered the loss of two children: her oldest, Charles in 1991 from a stroke and Miles, the third son from throat cancer from asbestos dust in 1996.

As my parents aged, they faced the same challenges that all do. Father slowed down considerably, and he could not rage as he used to. My dad died in the hospital from throat cancer caused by asbestos dust and Parkinson's disease in 1984. His mind held up and when I went home in 1982 for a visit, I confronted him about all the abuse. He owned it all. "I was a son of a bitch, wasn't I? I gave everything to my boys and it is my daughters who are taking care of me." We both had a healing experience.

I was the only one of 8 children to have had this experience with my father. I gave the eulogy at his funeral. My mother passed January, 22, 1999. She would have been 91 on the 23rd. She died at home with Carolyn and Marjorie in attendance. She always wanted to die in her home and she made it happen. I wrote the eulogy for her

141

and her granddaughter delivered it. Carolyn was the reason my parents lived as long as they did. She took diligent care of them. A short while after dad died, mother signed the home over to Carolyn. They died debt free and owning their home.

Mother found ways to move through her later years. She was always a reader and devoured books. She continued to crochet and taught herself how to knit. Lastly, she had several years of peace which she richly deserved.

Susan May Kuchinsky was born in Noxen, Pennsylvania, at home in 1946. She was the seventh of eight children and the only one to go to college. She had determined by the third grade that she wanted to be a teacher, and with the help of mother, brother, and counselor she made it happen. Her mother named her after brown-eyed susans, the flower, and it was her mother's name as well.

Susan started teaching high school classes in psychology and sociology in 1970. She earned a master's degree in guidance and counseling in 1979 at the University of Missouri, Kansas City, and an education specialist degree in 1986 from University of Missouri, Kansas City. With these credentials she became a school counselor in 1989 and retired in 2012 after 42 years in education. Throughout this career she remembered the advice her mother gave her after supplying the little boy with pennies, "Treat people fairly and love children."

WE ARE OUR MOTHERS' DAUGHTERS

9

Grow Old Gracefully

KATHLEEN LEONA SCHNEIDER
1921 to present

By Cheryl Moran

She picked up her broom and swept the crumbs away, the first breakfast was over. It was 6:00 a.m. Her father, Felix, and five-year old brother, Marvin, had already left the house to milk the cows and feed the horses, pigs and chickens. Kathleen, or Kak as she was later nick-named, was three years old. There was no time to play.

Mother Lena taught this oldest daughter how to run a farmhouse. Together they cleared the dishes and scrubbed the kitchen. And then it was time to get ready for the main 8 a.m. breakfast and take care of Baby Aurelia. Mother Lena brewed the coffee in a white chipped enamel coffee pot that burbled and spat on the black wood stove. Kak gathered eggs from the hen house and barn by herself in

145

the dark. She hated that because the hens sometimes bit her. Then she and her mother set the table again with homemade bread and jams in bowls. Then Kak ran to the milk house and fetched a pan of butter and a pint of milk for the cereal and toast. How much can a three-year-old girl carry, after all? Lena expertly tossed bacon and fried the eggs. Father and son returned for the morning family feast stomping the mud from their boots in the mud room. The daily routine on this busy family farm in the hills of Missouri, just 12 miles west of St. Charles, had still hardly begun. Like most days, the routine of meals, field work, tending to gardens, home and other chores would not end until well after dark.

The year was 1924. The family had electricity but not indoor plumbing. Felix and Lena had bought the land less than a decade earlier and were beginning to build a farm that would be the pride of their life. The home they lived in was fairly new, built by Felix with the help of family and neighbors. In time, Felix added other structures, including a barn for his dairy business, an ice house to store ice through the summer months, a corn crib, a chicken coop, a butcher house used to hang the meat and store his annual wine, and sheds for his tractor and farm implements. In some ways, it seemed like a rich existence. But the family never had the luxury of feeling rich. The times were tough and money was scarce. Economically, the Schneider family often struggled, but they raised a family that shared a deep love for each other, their extended family, their community and their religion.

Like so many families, the Schneiders had a member of a previous generation living with them. Kak's Grandma Roeper needed to be fed. She ate only ice cream, likely because a stroke had left her unable to tolerate anything else. The doctor had probably suggested this as a way to keep her alive and the family obeyed. Her diet forced the family to create ice cream year around. Marvin, my Uncle Bud, Kak's older brother, laboriously churned the ice cream machine day after day after month, season in, season out. Later Kak took over the task each day, and later still she passed it on to her younger siblings Aurelia and Jim. The youngest sibling, lucky Mary Jean, never had this chore because Grandma finally died before the last child was burdened with the task.

Kak memorized the ice cream recipe of milk, cream, eggs, sugar and vanilla – mostly products from the dairy farm. She and Uncle Bud were the ones who fed the ice cream to Grandma Roeper in her bedroom three times a day. Only Uncle Bud had the distinguished position of sometimes receiving attention from Grandma as she told him how smart he was. Uncle Bud glowed in this praise while his siblings looked on, for he was mentally disabled and desperately needed her encouragement. Encouraging words were sparse in this German culture where hard work was honored because it was a matter of survival and pride, over the need for endearing statements. Mental toughness was emphasized.

Winters brought stark cold to the eastern Missouri farm. My Grandpa Felix got up early to warm the house before everyone else got up by shoveling anthracite coal into the furnace. Of course, only the first floor of the two-story home was heated and it took a while to do that, so winter mornings were frosty as the children prepared for school. They could see their breath as they jumped from warm bed to cold clothes and ran down the stairs to the comparative warmth of the kitchen. A quick splash of icy water from the pump at the sink across the face, a finger full of Pepsodent tooth powder across the teeth, and to the table for oatmeal, eggs, bacon, toast. They did not spend much time in the outhouse either!

The winters also brought opportunities. Making ice cream daily meant that they needed a supply of ice year-round. Grandpa would harvest ice from rivers and lakes! Once the ice was about one-foot-deep in January or February, he would use a saw to cut blocks to store them. Pulling the horse and wagon onto the lake, he hoisted with ice tongs 25-50 pound chunks of ice onto the wagon, run the horses up the bank and on to the ice house on the farm There he placed into the prepared well of dirt each frozen cube and covered them with sawdust and/or hay to preserve them through the summer. By harvest time in September or October the supply had dwindled to one block left. How they made ice cream between then and the next harvest must have been dicey.

My Grandma Lena took great pride in her large truck garden of lettuces and radishes, onions, red beets and beans, grapes and raspberries, tomatoes and potatoes, turnips and cucumbers, cabbage

147

for sauerkraut, pumpkins. (As a young child, I remember the sweet smell of digging in this good, rich dirt.) Cherries, peaches, plums and apples were gathered from the orchard for Grandma's delicious pies and jams, for storing in pint jars. All of the plants and trees needed care. There was no waste in time or materials. Every member of the family was needed and every member worked hard to maintain the farm. They rose before dawn each day to start the long list of chores. Good discipline was a matter of survival.

Kak said she thought that she was born with a dust cloth in her hands. "You do what needs to be done." Either Grandma or Grandpa took an ax to the chickens. Corn, wheat and soy beans moved from furrow to pan and fed the animals. Grandpa and Uncle Bud milked a herd of 25 or so cows by hand and sold the milk. Kak and her younger sister Aurelia enjoyed planting the flowers around the house each spring; marigolds were her favorite. The smell of fragrant lilacs and pale pink roses was a source of joy and beauty for the family. Grandpa loved farming, always learning and trying new methods from the farm co-op. Grandma loved cooking with her special butterscotch pie being a favorite.

Kak helped her mother care for the three younger children as they came along plus the grandmother, still lying abed upstairs depending on her thrice a day ice cream diet. Family members helped each other. Grandpa Felix helped two of Grandma Lena's sisters and their families when they suffered the early deaths of their husbands. One aunt found shoe factory work and moved to St. Charles. The other did housework but it was often not enough to make the ends meet. Felix would cut wood to keep his sister-in-law's family warm. He and Grandma Lena shared groceries to keep them fed. Then the larger family including these aunts would gather in the fall on Grandpa's farm when it came time for putting up silage of hard corn and grasses, butchering the pig and making apple butter in a huge, black cauldron. At this fall gathering, the women worked together in the morning to prepare a huge lunch for all the workers. There was lots of laughter and story-telling that day.

The children attended the Catholic Assumption elementary school that was a little more than one mile from the farm. They walked both ways every day. The Catholic Church was central to the

148

immigrant German community. It helped the community come together and support each other. It was the foundation of their lives, giving them hope. Uncle Bud stopped going to school after sixth grade but he did learn to read, an accomplishment for him and a compliment to the family for valuing him in that way. Kak regretfully stopped going to school after eighth grade because her family could not spare her being in school any longer than that. She was heartbroken.

Kak and her mother-in-law Urilla vowed to make that up to the women in the family and began saving to send me to college when I was in high school. They felt they owed the family a college educated daughter for the sacrifice that had had to make in the lean years.

But Kak also found time for fun. She learned how to play softball, and was one of the few girls in her town that owned a softball mitt. Her favorite part was playing short-stop or catcher. She was a competent horse rider, and loved to sing and dance. To my great surprise, I also learned much later in life that my mother had a wild side. She loved to ride on the back of some of her friends' motorcycles and feel her hair blowing in the wind.

When Kak was 17 years old, Grandpa Felix sent her to St. Charles to care for his bed-ridden Mother Schneider (my great grandmother), who had broken her hip. Kak initially took over the upkeep of her grandmother's house and shared the care of her grandmother's health with her uncle and eventually other grandchildren. She told me that she felt inadequate for the job but she persevered. Her dad knew that she could assume this responsibility. He believed in her. After about two years, Kak moved back to the farm and another of Grandpa Felix's many nieces took Kak's place. Grandpa Felix came from a large family of nine boys and one girl. After Kak returned to the farm, she took a job in St. Charles at the shoe heel plant. She traveled back and forth from the farm as did many other girls to the factory.

While in St. Charles Kak met her husband-to-be, Bob Buse, at a dance where he played the trumpet in a band. Kak loved to dance and listen to music. Dances were a favorite pastime for both city and country teenagers and they would travel miles to hear the bands play their favorite tunes. Bob loved to play music but did not enjoy dancing as much in those first years. As he aged, he learned to love dancing, as he accompanied Kak to dances on a regular basis into their 80s. They did not try to be anyone other than themselves. Kak believed that she was good enough. It was part of respecting herself, of growing old gracefully.

As part of the war effort, Kak took a chance and applied for a job at the Curtiss-Wright plant in St. Louis as an A-25 Shrike dive bomber riveter. She worked for this company both before and after she married in 1943. Bob enlisted in the navy and was shortly transferred to the Sausalito, California area. He found a live-in job for Kak as a cook and housekeeper while he waited for deployment. After deployment, Kak moved back to O'Fallon again. I asked her why she gave up living in the beautiful city of Sausalito. She told me that "family is so much more important than place".

Dad in 1943

While on the lengthy, three-day train trip back home, she lost a pregnancy. Luckily, there was one other young woman on the train who would buy sanitary napkins for mom when the train stopped, to help stop the bleeding.

During World War II, the trains mainly transported the troops, so few women were on board. Bob's mother and sister met her at the train station and cared for her until she was ready to go back to the farm. She was mortified that anyone had to take care of her. She did not speak of this tragedy for more than 30 years. I first learned about it from my aunt. During World War II, many people believed in the tough attitude of silent endurance or "a stiff upper lip" as they called it. Kak was independent and wanted no one to feel sorry for her. She would endure. She felt confident in herself. She was a fighter. Her heroine was Katharine Hepburn, the actress who was tough and wore pants instead of dresses.

Mom and Dad's wedding reception at the farm: Grandpa Felix and Grandma Lena Schneider, Mom and Dad, Grandma Urilla and Grandpa Bob Buse

After the war, Kak and Bob had another baby but Wayne died in childbirth with the umbilical cord wrapped around his neck, a second tragedy for the couple. Then in 1948, they gave birth to me, Cheryl Kay, on a hot August day in a hospital filled with crying babies and no air conditioning. I suffered a broken arm and an ugly cyst to the head, caused by an angry nurse who dropped me. One too many babies cried for their mothers that day. Mom and Dad carried me on a pillow with my cast until my arm healed. We kept the cast for many years near my scrapbook as proof of the violence.

In November of 1950, my brother David was born. Until David started kindergarten, he was called "boy baby" by family because I had so named him in the womb. I wanted a brother. I dearly loved

Mom laughing at sister, Aurelia's, wedding, 1941   **Dad and Mom's Wedding 1943**

him and thought that he was mine, at least to boss around. David did not appreciate that intention, however, and we fought a lot when we were small.

Dad loved to talk with people and became quite a good traveling salesman. Mom stayed at home, trying to prove herself to her mother-in-law, Urilla Buse, that she could keep a perfect house. It was a German expectation that the wife maintained an immaculate home. Mom did this very well, working hard to be the perfect mom, accomplishing her goal of management. While the home looked perfect, time spent with us children was not a priority. She wanted us to play by ourselves, an activity that she had not enjoyed as a child. She was good at directing but not good at hugging or cuddling, listening or

David, 1956

spending time with us. Every day she demanded perfection from us and every day she displayed great anger when the goal was missed.

She had to raise us mostly by herself while dad traveled until I was ten or eleven years old. She felt judged in the city, isolated. Luckily, her siblings and their families gathered every weekend on the Schneider farm, with all the grandchildren present. She was accepted on the farm, but not, she thought, in the city. She was seen as unsophisticated at first in the city, but her down-to-earth approach gave her wisdom. She maintained her self-confidence even with competitive siblings who became wealthy and considered themselves superior to our family. Mom's sister-in-law was married to a man who became a bank president and belonged to country clubs. One of her sisters married a man who eventually became quite wealthy in the engineering field. Through it all, Mom maintained her identity.

Dad felt entitled as a man, that home responsibility was not an expectation for him. He was a city-born son, one who felt that he should rule. His mother, my Grandma Urilla, was raised in a household whose father died when the children were still young. Grandma Urilla's dad had owned a hardware store in the late 1800s and early 1900s. Grandma Urilla's mother did not have the legal right to own the store. Women did not have the right to vote or own property at that time. Because of this, the oldest male who was seven years younger than my grandma, was needed to sign legal

Jim, 1966

papers for the hardware store and act as the family representative. This son was treated as special because he was so needed to sign documents.

All the children helped to run the store, but my Grand Uncle Mick held a special position. He was allowed to call the shots and dad greatly admired him and wanted to be like him. But Grandmother Urilla was strong and she became a suffragette, supporting women's right to vote. Shortly before my Grandma Urilla died in 1978, she told me that her greatest disappointment was that she did not live long enough to see a woman president.

Before I turned 10-years-old and David eight, Mom experienced tragic losses of her mother, father and beloved brother within a two-year time frame. This tragedy was heightened by the fact that she served as executor of the will and had to manage the farm and her brother, Uncle Bud's care. It took a long time for mom's siblings to agree to sell the farm to help care for Uncle Bud and to get from under the burden of managing a rental property that the farm had become.

Mom kept herself busy at home. Eventually, she became part of a club that played cards and made enduring friends. She was able to talk her husband into buying an old 1950 Plymouth so that she had transportation when he was out of town. It was unusual to have two cars in one family in the 1950s. She felt liberated, for she had learned to drive on the farm when she was 14 years old, and it felt good to be in control. Mom was an excellent home manager, paying bills and running the house so that it always looked and ran perfectly. Her cooking skills were legendary, especially appreciated by all family members and visiting friends. Mom never sat still. Even at night, she crocheted or continued with household tasks. She seldom watched television or read a book.

Top to bottom:
Brother Dave, Mom, and wife Marge;
Mom and Cheryl, 2014;
Mom, 2011;
Cheryl's husband, Terry, and Mom, 2013; and,
Jim, wife Rita, Maura, Paul, Joseph, Mom & Terry, 2008

WE ARE OUR MOTHERS' DAUGHTERS

When I was in high school another son, Jim, was born. Before he was in first grade, Mom found a job as a seamstress. The extra income was saved and later used to help put me through college. It was a particular point of pride for Grandma Urilla and Mom to send me, a girl, to college because neither of them got to finish school. While in her 50s, Grandma Urilla went to school and became an LPN and worked until she was 77 years old. Mom worked many years as a cook for the public school system and retired when she was 63 years old.

In retirement, she kept busy volunteering in the hospital gift shop and at church fundraisers as the cashier. She quilted with a ladies group and loved to bowl. She finally quit bowling at age 86. She and dad loved to travel and they went to Hawaii and Europe, as well as to Florida most winters. They loved being around family and often housed visiting family. They had many friends.

Mom is currently living at age 95 at Lake St. Charles Retirement Village in St. Charles, Missouri, and is still active. She can still do math in her head quickly. Though her memory is challenged at this point, she participates in activities such as bingo and group exercising in the assisted care area. She walks briskly with her walker. She tells me now that to grow old gracefully means to take life as it comes, and to try not to get too frustrated. She is content. She does not have to please anyone other than herself and she is kind to those around her. Her secret to contentment - pray often and have faith in Jesus.

The Catholic Church was always important to Mom and Dad. Mom's oldest ancestor in the United States emigrated in the 1830s from Germany and the whole family remained Catholic as part of a strong spiritual community. German was spoken in the community until World War I, when it stopped because the government was wary there might be German spies in the St. Charles community. Dad's German family heritage goes as far back as the 1840s and again the importance of the Catholic faith sustained his family. Faith in God helped them to endure many hardships.

As I have evolved my perspective and understanding over the years, I have gotten a much deeper grasp how difficult life was for Mom. But Mom would never tell me or even herself that such was the case. I now realize that Mom is the strongest person I have ever known.

Cheryl Moran is a family historian of the Buse/Schneider family, the family into which she was born. She has collected stories and numerous pictures over the years, documenting special occasions. This article is a tribute to one Missouri farm family in both prosperous and hard economic times, and to the life of one small-town family after World War II. The story begins in the 1920s, goes through the Depression, World War II, and post-war era. It continues to this day as Kak is 95 years old and still active.

Cheryl graduated with a B.A. in math and elementary education from Lindenwood University in St. Charles, Missouri, in 1970. She was married shortly after graduation to Terry Moran, who worked as a manager for Stix Baer and Fuller department store in St. Louis. She began her career as a second grade teacher and taught for seven years until they moved to Kansas City for Terry's job in insurance sales for Delta Dental where he eventually became a vice president. Using her math skills, she worked for Burns and McDonnell as an engineering technician and in similar venues. Cheryl prides herself in offering her math skills as a volunteer to people who need tax preparation, managing three centers at one time making sure that people got their taxes prepared properly for free.

In her later years Cheryl has acquired a reputation as a fine oil and pastel painter, jewelry maker and designer. Her mother Kak looks at her daughter's life and says, "You have it made," but it was Kak who made it possible. As Kak aged gracefully so has Cheryl.

ACKNOWLEDGEMENTS
and an INVITATION

Thank you to all who contributed to this first volume…from Hillary Clinton and her inspiration, to the authors, and my friend, David W. Jackson, who stepped up to help edit and design this book on a tight deadline. I'm already looking forward to future volumes of "We are Our Mothers' Daughters."

Women unite. Let's stand up and represent to girls and women of today…and in the future…that we are our mothers' daughters. We have something to impart for posterity about having lived as women gaining independence in the 20th and early 21st centuries. The fight is not over.

Future volumes for Last Lap Press in this series will be about other brave women. When we get 10 stories for each category we will publish the volume. Ask your friends and relatives to submit their stories as well.

1) World War I. Does your family have stories from that era? Grandmothers? Great aunts?
2) We will assemble stories of women in World War II: Was your mother a World War II nurse? Rosie the Riveter? How did women of the Greatest Generation in your family survive and thrive through tough times? The Home Front? Victory Gardens?
3) Another volume we'll build is women in male professional jobs, engineering, medicine, science. How did your mother survive, train, excel in a male-dominated field?
4) Stories about pioneer women: Look back over your family history.
5) How good an ancestry.com genealogist are you? Do you have any family stories about ancestral mothers that you have always wanted to commit to paper and haven't?

WE ARE OUR MOTHERS' DAUGHTERS

Now's your time!

Go way back—even to the Old Country if you have a fully-fleshed story to tell.

If you are a mother or daughter, you are hereby invited to submit a tribute to your mother. Share her successes in spite of what life may have thrown at her. Tell readers how you were inspired and uplifted by that special woman.

Your submission of text and accompanied imagery may be compiled by Last Lap Press, in future published tributes titled, "We Are Our Mother's Daughters." Here are some simple guidelines:

1) E-mail to weareourmothersdaughters@gmail.com .wpd electronic file from 7-10, single-spaced pages on your mother's life, that includes at least one or two paragraphs at the end about YOU. Include factual, historical narrative and inspirational advice to convey who she was, what she experienced, and how she impacted and/or molded you.

2) Place her full name (including her maiden and married name(s)) and complete birth (and death, if appropriate) dates at the top of your manuscript, followed by your name and contact information (name, physical mailing address, e-mail address and phone number).
   The title of your piece will be a quote that either she coined, used, or describes her.

3) Include up to four (4), publishable digital images of your mother, plus one (1) of yourself.

4) Submit manuscript. Include a $100 nonrefundable submission fee at the time text and images are transferred. The entry fee covers review for possible publication, editing and designing.

5) Your submission of text and images, when transferred comes with your understood permission to publish, and will be "printed with permission." You will be notified when the next edition of, "We Are Our Mothers' Daughters," is published.

Send to:

Last Lap Press
weareourmothersdaughters@gmail.com
(Invoices issued from Paypal from this e-mail)

facebook.com/weareourmothersdaughters

CPSIA information can be obtained
at www.ICGtesting.com
Printed in the USA
LVHW052204081019
633637LV00016B/805/P